THE STORY OF THE

Q1s

The story of the
Q1s

John Scott Morgan

In memory of Jack Heath

One of the Southern's youngest drivers
And who worked with John Pelham Maitland
At Nine Elms

KRB Publications
2 Denewulf Close
BISHOPS WALTHAM
Hants
SO32 1GZ

Printed by the Amadeus Press

ISBN 0954485912

Front cover:
33010 at Hither Green, August 1959.   *Colour Rail.*

Rear cover - top:
33006, by now officially withdrawn, but seen approaching Southampton Terminus, 19 March 1966.   *A. Molyneaux.*

Rear cover - lower:
The LCGB 'New Forester' railtour of 19 March 1966, with 33006 at Lyndhurst Road.   *J.E. Bell.*

Title page:
33003 regaining the Southern lines east of Reading having collected an inter-regional freight at Scours Lane and probably destined for Redhill.   *Brian Davis Collec.*

Opposite:
Brand new at Brighton in 1942. The first of the class complete with 'sunshine lettering', a style which may not have appeared on all other members.   *NRM / BTC 420/68*

Contents

C16 at Eastleigh. The engine is basically in 'as-built' condition including the take off drive to the mechanical lubricators. Smokebox handrails were not fitted to C1 as built, but certainly appeared later. It may be that later members of the class were so equipped from new. This particular engine may also have been unique in having had shutters fitted the cab side windows for a period. By 1947 though, standard apertures had appeared. P.Ransome Wallis 11823 / NRM

C21 at Eastleigh. Built at Ashford in 1942, this engine was renumbered by BR as 33021 in November 1950.

Tony Sedgwick

INTRODUCTION

I have always liked Q1s, ever since as a two year old, I was startled by one as it crossed the level crossing at Bollo Lane, Acton, while hauling a cross-London freight from Willesden to Feltham yard. Those clanking, churning box pox wheels and the sheer bulk of the boiler and cab left a lasting impression on me.

There is nothing beautiful about Q1s. They are probably the most ugly steam locomotive ever built, but for all that, they are certainly very impressive, and probably the most powerful 0-6-0 tender goods ever constructed. In outward looks, they were not unlike a Hornby MO series clockwork 'O' gauge tin plate locomotive. One might think that the drawing office at Binns Road, Liverpool and Eastleigh came to some secret agreement.

During my childhood years, I had quite a few encounters with the class, primarily at Reading, where the class were a common sight on Reading-Tonbridge line services.

The railway staff called them 'Spam-cans', or 'Charlies'; the enthusiasts called them 'coffee pots'. I loved to watch them leaving Reading South with a set of Bullied carriage stock, and heading out towards Earley and Wokingham on the first leg of the journey to Guildford. I have heard many stories of the class over the years, but some of the best stories came from the late Jack Heath - a driver based at Guildford who had a lot of experience with them.

He once told me about a horrendous journey with a Q1 from Tonbridge to Reading, with an overloaded train. The 0-6-0 kept on trying to hunt its way off the track, as a result of the sheer weight of the load. Eventually, the train arrived at Reading, some three quarters of an hour late and Jack was glad to hand the stock over to the Western Region.

One further story he told me was of a WR fireman who wanted to learn the road to Redhill. A Reading based Western crew often worked over this route with Manor class 4-6-0s and 53XX 2-6-0s, the young fireman approached Jack at Reading South and asked him if he would allow him to ride to Guildford on the footplate with him. Jack had no objection, so the fireman jumped up into the cab, and presently they started off to Guildford. As they passed Reading South depot, and ran through Earley, the Western fireman started to make comments about the Q1. "Funny looking thing; looks more like a clockwork engine; you don't have many cab fittings do you; what sort of brakes has this thing got?"

Jack Heath pointed out that the designer, Mr Bullied, had, for good reason, designed it that way and that although funny looking to his Western eyes, the Q1 had a much higher tractive effort than all the 0-6-0 and 2-6-0 types on the Western Region.

After a few more funny remarks from the Western guest, Jack decided to have some fun with him. The Q1 was already bowling along at a decent speed, so Jack opened the regulator a few extra notches. The locomotive then started to lurch from side to side and hunt along the track. The Western fireman became very alarmed, "This thing can't be safe; let me off at the next station; I can't stand any more of this!" The next station was Wokingham, which was reached a few minutes later.

As the fireman jumped down from the footplate, he turned and said to Jack, "Thank God for that! That thing is not safe. There should be a law against a thing like that; it should not be allowed; its got no brakes!" Jack and his fireman watched the unhappy Western fireman head for the footbridge on the other platform. They looked at each other and laughed like drains.

One further story which deserves relating concerns a driver at Guildford, who loved practical jokes. He not only played these on his workmates, but also the public at large. One morning, during the rush hour, he was working a freight from Guildford for Nine Elms goods yard with a Q1. As the train approached Woking, the driver turned to his fireman and said, "Just watch this now". He then put his driver's cap back to front, proceeded to stick his false teeth out, whilst grimacing his face, and leered out of the cab. The result of all this had to be seen to be believed. Passengers on the platform almost fell over in horror and several women screamed with shock.

The Q1s were a class that brought out the best and worst in all kinds of people. They were the product of a remarkable man and his design team.

Oliver Bullied was an engineer who often thought the unthinkable. Sometimes it worked, as with the Q1s and sometimes it proved to be less than satisfactory, as with the 0-6-0 diesel shunter, the plastic utility van and the "Leader".

The Q1 was a remarkable locomotive that would have had several off-shoot designs, had original plans taken place. Certainly there were plans for a 0-6-4 tank version and even an austerity Pacific was envisaged. As it was, only the Q1s became a reality. This is their story.

ACKNOWLEDGEMENTS

I would like to thank the following for their help in the compilation of this volume: Hugh Abbinnett, J.H. Aston, B. Barnard, J. Bell, L. Bowles, R C. Casserley, B. Curl, A.J. Fry, E. Gamblin, A. Goodyear, A. Gosling, N. Hamshere. R. Hope, B. Kimber, Lens of Sutton, A. Molyneaux, F. Moss, The Curator and Staff at the National Railway Museum, J.D. Preston, J. Scrace, A. Sedgewick, R. Stumpf. H.F. Wheeler, E.A Woolard, T. Wright, and M. York.

Cab view as originally built. Bulleid's concern for ease of operation for the crew is as obvious here as it was on the Pacifics. The major controls for the driver and fireman kept separate whenever possible. Even so, further thought could have been given such as angled front windows to avoid glare and a lubricator which did not poke the driver in the eye when he removed the side drain plug to release any water prior to refilling with oil. This latter feature is not obvious from the photograph. As will be gathered from the position of the regulator, the engine could be driven from either side, although applying the brake could only be done from the left hand side.

1	Reversing gear	7b	Boiler water gauge
2	Combined brake (steam and vacuum, application and ejector controls)	8	Regulator
3	Blower	9	Steam heat gauge
4	Combined Vacuum gauges	10	Lubricators
5	Boiler pressure gauge	11	Sanding gear
6	Injector steam valves and steam manifold valves	12	Injector water valves
7a	Boiler water gauge		

NRM 42/82

Chapter 1

THE CONCEPT OF A 'SPAM-CAN'

After the delivery of the last Schools class 4-4-0 in 1935, the Southern Railway Board decided to keep a stringent eye on any money available for steam locomotive construction. The reason for this was so that any future expenditure should be directed at electrification projects. Only direct replacements for old and worn out steam locomotives, or projects to replace a group of old obsolete designs with a smaller group of locomotives were considered.

At the time of Richard Maunsell's retirement in 1937, a project to build a class of twenty 0-6-0 tender goods locomotives was in hand. These machines were classified as Q class and were designed to replace ex-LSWR "Jubilee" A12 0-4-2 tender locomotives which had been used as mixed traffic locomotives since the grouping in 1923.

Each member of the Q class would cost £7200 each, when ordered in March 1936. They were designed to be paired with second-hand 3500 gallon tenders at the time when Oliver Bullied took over from Richard Maunsell in 1937. There were reservations raised by Bullied and his team over the project to build the twenty Q class 0-6-0s. Bullied referred to the class as pedestrian and old fashioned.

The Q class locomotives were built between January 1938 and September 1939, but they proved less than satisfactory in traffic and over the decades from 1939 until 1965, when the last members of the class were withdrawn, numerous modifications were made to improve their performance.

In the early dates of the Second World War, Oliver Bullied had to consider whether to build more Qs, or design something more modern and to his liking. By 1940, at the time of "operation Dynamo" (the evacuation of the British Expeditionary Force from Dunkirk), the Board of the Southern Railway and the operating department sent a memo to Oliver Bullied, asking for more 0-6-0 goods locomotives to cover the increase in freight and military traffic.

The design that spawned the Q1 class, a Maunsell Q class loco of 1938. Popular culture has it that Bulleid arrived just too late to prevent construction, although in practice this was perhaps not so likely as only one set of frames had been cut by the end of 1937. More likely is the fact that the design was accepted as likely to be robust and reliable and which was indeed the case even if they lacked the apparent charisma of Bulleid's own designs.   *Curl Collec.*

The answer for Bullied and his design team was to start from scratch, almost to think the unthinkable, to produce a totally new design, geared to the needs of the Southern in wartime. The result which emerged during the next eighteen months was a design that would shock, amaze and even anger some of the more traditional locomotive designers. Sir William Stanier even remarked when he was shown a photograph of the prototype C1, "Where do you put the key?". The brutal lines of the Q1, with its lack of running plate, its boiler cladding design that to any layman looked like a collection of Spam or corn beef cans welded together, and its square-looking smoke box had "austerity" stamped all over it. The box-pok wheels gave them character and somehow, these 0-6-0 monsters grew on people, both the operating staff and the public.

The design of the Q1 by the Bullied design team was almost the *bauhaus* approach to locomotive production - basic, simple and brutal. Work on the Q1 project had started in earnest in 1941, the main criteria for the design being as follows: firstly, to produce a locomotive with the largest possible boiler - hence the use of the 'Lord Nelson' flanging blocks; secondly, to pay special attention to the cylinders' passages and motion to make the locomotive as free running as possible for mixed traffic use; and thirdly, to produce a machine with a weight of 51 tons, this being $1\frac{1}{2}$ tons heavier than the existing Q class design.

It was very important to produce a locomotive that had greater power than the Q, with a higher tractive effort, but which at the same time, did not turn out to be overweight, which would have defeated the object of the project.

The new locomotives had Stephenson's motion designed to give six 6" travel, and good valve events in both forward and reverse running. The possibility of enclosing the motion in an oil bath was looked at, but was quickly rejected owing to the lack of space available. The boiler was designed to run at 220 psi, which was increased to 230 psi at the design stage, and the steam reverser was of a Drummond LSWR design. The cladding for the boiler was produced using an early form of fibreglass classed 'Idaglass', which was attached on a square steel framework constructed around the boiler. This is what gave rise to the square "Span-can" look.

The locomotives had rounded enclosed cabs, with a flexible canvas connection between the locomotive and tender, which also had a cab to protect the crew when the locomotive ran in reverse. The large six-wheeled tender which also had box-pok wheels, held 3700 gallons of water and five tons of coal.

When outshopped, the prototype C1 weighted $51\frac{1}{4}$ tons. It performed very well during trials, which involved test trains of various weights, over varying gradients of line. The Q1s ran freely in both directions up to a maximum of 75 mph, or at much slower speeds on heavy trains or when shunting.

There were reservations about the locomotives' lack of a running plate, which Bullied responded to by conducting trails with a Q1 at speed in both directions. Some of the locomotive crews had complained about the sight of the connecting rods revolving at speed without a running plate to protect the footplate crew in the event of a connecting rod being thrown through the cab.

Oliver Bullied allayed their fears by riding on a Q1 at speed himself. There were problems, however, with braking on heavy trains, especially on downward inclines, as the brake gear was based on that used on the Q class. This led to a series of trials between Basingstoke and Eastleigh, which took place in 1943.

A Q1 and a Maunsell S15 4-6-0 were used for the braking trials. There were some hair-raising moments when the Q1, with a train of unfitted wagons weighing 900 tons, was pushed along at 45 mph, even after a full brake application. It took over three miles to stop the train, and as a result, the train ran past a home signal at danger when passing Wallers Ash, and continued for a mile after the signal.

On the other hand, the S15 4-6-0, on a similar train could stop in a distance of $1\frac{3}{4}$ miles. As a result of this, the Q1 0-6-0s were limited to 55 mph although they often ran at faster speeds, thus harking back to the early 75 mph trails.

As a result of thin metal being used on the tender tanks and outer plates, the tenders were prone to leak water. This was due to buckling when in daily use. Also, at first, the lubricators gave problems which had to be resolved, in order to give the pistons and valves better performance. The first member of the class, numbered C1, was out shopped in March 1942 from Brighton, to a mixed reception from the technical press, as we have already seen.

For all the remarks made by people who often did not understand the reason for its design, or the engineering concept behind it, the Q1s were the most powerful 0-6-0 tender locomotive ever built. For that reason, and many more, the new Q1s would prove their worth and value, at a time of crisis unparalleled in world history.

Eventually, there would be forty members of the class, numbered C1 to C40. There were proposals to build further austerity type locomotives. Designs were prepared for an 0-6-4T, a 4-6-4T and an austerity Pacific. Also, one of the two proposals for replacement 0-6-0Ts for Southampton Docks was to be a Q1 based design.

In the event, none of the proposed designs left the drawing board and the Q1 was the only member of the austerity family to see the light of day.

Chapter 2

'ON THE ROAD' - Hugh Abbinnett

I'd like you to accompany me on a trip with a 'Charlie', but an introduction would perhaps be in order first. As this is a night ride, our way to the grimy monster is lit by an oil-plumed paraffin 'duck' lamp. Three precarious steel steps take us up the towering black side to the footplate. From the spacious wooden-floored cab we shall endeavor once more to satisfy the constant craving for tons of coal, and countless gallons of water, of a Bulleid Q1 steam locomotive.

The Q1s were designed as an austerity measure to assist the smooth running of the railways during the 1939-45 hostilities. The Bulleid regime decided that, being somewhat of an improvement on the Maunsell Qs, the Q1s would be numbered in a more flamboyant manner. The numerals therefore, were prefixed by the letter 'C'. What finer material for the quick-witted cleaner, fireman, or driver, than 'C' for Charlie, and thus they swiftly became known throughout the entire Southern Region. Enginemen in cabins as far apart as Dover and Exeter, endlessly discussed the attributes and failings oft he newly-introduced 'Charlies'.

The most apparent and glaring omission from Mr. Bulleid's design, was the precious framing, or walkway, above the six huge 'Boxpok' driving wheels, around which drivers displayed the merits of their craft to anyone who cared to observe - skilful ministration of lubricants to missionary boxes, links and glands, and the like. "If they want me to climb up there they've got another think coming. They'll just have to run hot won't 'em."

Concern for the difficulties of the driver, as in all things, must come first, but what of the poor, lesser mortal - the chief 'dogsbody' of all time - the ever present, uncomplaining fireman? Feeling ran high about cleaning out smokeboxes, while precariously perched on a steel strip, which measured about 1 foot by 4 foot. Peculiar as this operation was to Western men. Southern crews always cleaned their own fires and smokeboxes. So, to add to the unsavory task of removing about six or seven barrow-loads of dusty (and sometimes red-hot smokebox ashes) the 3/4" inch nuts holding the smokebox retaining lugs, would

Freshly renumbered, 33018 at Eastleigh on 12 August 1949. This engine would appear to have been unique in having an extended handrail fitted to one side of the smokebox. It is not known if this was retained throughout its life. Notice the open side door to the cab. Commencing in 1946 these had been lengthened downwards, which, together with other modifications to the tender, reduced the incidence of complaints due to side draughts when running tender-first.

On the very duty for which Bulleid had intended the class. 33032 near to Edenbridge in July 1956.   Photomatic

assume a severe reluctance to be slackened to allow the door to be swung open for cleaning. Many a poor unfortunate ended up waist-deep in ashes, having stepped back into a void where the front framing on more familiar engines used to be.

The first engines to arrive at the depots were fitted with the 'Eureka' type water displacement lubricators, a massive brass object suspended from a bracket in the corner, just inboard of the fireman's side window. The large 'T' shaped brass drainage key cleared the window by a mere fraction of an inch. This tyrannical device introduced the ill-famed malady of 'Charlie's Eye', which was a severe gash in the near vicinity of the left eye, caused by the quick withdrawal of the head from the open window, to impale the undefended eye area upon the newly-cast sharp key. This painful experience was done away with by introducing mechanical lubricators on the later engines.

Putting smokebox cleaning well behind us ("Thank God", as we used to say), the next auspicious job was to clean the fire, a job not made easy by Mr. Bulleid's concern

for our protection when running in a rearward direction. High sides and an all-enveloping roof over the cab were hardly instrumental in assisting the manipulation of an eleven-foot long shovel, fully laden with red-hot clinker and smoking coals. Negotiate shovel into firehole door, fill it, then steer to the opening at the cab side of the loco and drop it onto the ground. This was the theory, when all went well, but with the slightest deviation, the shovel was jarred, and clinker deposited on the cab's wooden floor. Net result was a roaring inferno at your leather-clad feet, necessitating a hasty application of water from the 'pet pipe' to douse the flames, and the sweeping of ashes from the footplate. This soul-destroying operation didn't make an already precarious love-hate relationship between locomotive and fireman any easier of course. Even more abrasives were added to the constant duel.

Not the least of these was the design innovation, on the earlier locos, of the tender filling orifices being placed very close to the entrance of the loco. Other loco types had a large-bore opening high on the extreme rear of the tender,

C17 being coaled at Eastleigh on 10 June 1948. This engine has already been attached to a modified tender as witness the position of the fireman holding the bag against the water pressure. (See also caption on page 59) R.S. Carpenter

and this was capable of accepting a flexible pipe of leather or rubber. The pipe could be laid along the steel plates, into the opening, and the heavy tender lid used as a weight to keep it in place, so allowing the busy fireman to go about some other task while the water level slowly rose. With the Bulleid side-entry fillers, the small-bore openings had to be watched constantly. Should the pipe overflow, or come out, it was always the fireman who got wet overalls and a wet shirt to last him the rest of the day.

Another constant reminder of the savings made in manufacturing the 'Charlies', was the draughty footplate flooring. When the ashpan was being raked, the fine, white ash rose up through the many cracks and openings, leaving a white dusting on anyone on the footplate. If the loco had been in service for some time, the ash level would rise in the hopper, and as the engine oscillated (as only a 'Charlie' could), the fine white powder crept up through the cracks and crannies, making the crew seated just three feet above, cough and splutter.

The saving graces of these 0-6-0 locos would probably have seemed few at the time, but looking back at some of the antiquated steam locomotives then in daily use, perhaps

the provision of an upholstered seat with a backrest was pretty revolutionary, after the nine-inch by nine-inch slab of hard wood fitted to a Drummond T9. The cab was all-enveloping, and its protection when running tender-first in adverse weather drew praise from normally frozen crews - there was no longer the necessity to turn railway-issue raincoats backwards to keep out freezing snow, sleet, or rain.

The driver's look-out came in for praise too, for perched high above the rapidly rotating connecting rods, the long slim glass window offered a clear view along the side of the boiler. Not admittedly, much of a view over the boiler, but then the alert fireman was expected to take care of any sightings needed on his side. 'Charlie' drivers soon found the most comfortable and relaxed position from which to drive. With back resting easily against the support, and feet placed on the adjacent steam-reverser frame, many rip-roaring miles on these 'ugly ducklings', born of austerity, were covered on both passenger and freight trains.

The 'Charlies' always seemed to virtually 'grab hold' of any length of freight train, and possibly because drivers of the 1942 era were rather impressed by their new 'steeds' with their 230 lbs per square inch pressure (as opposed to the 160 lbs. of an Adams 'Jubilee' 0-4-2), up to sixty loose-fitted wagons, with merely a light 'pillbox' brake van as brake power, would zoom out of Southern marshalling yards like rockets in the night.

On one such occasion, I was driving the 2.02 a.m. from Bevois Park Up Yard in September 1957. With sixty loose-coupled empty coal wagons behind, we stormed along, with steam pressure in the 'two hundreds'. Brilliant reflected light flashed up to the night sky, as my fireman slammed the long-bladed shovel on the rim of the firebox door, distributing coal to the distant corners of the firegrate.

As we charged up the rise to Eastleigh, the outer arm on the gantry at the exit from the Loco sheds displayed clear "Greens" on both its Stop and Distant quadrants. My fireman, as always, raised two fingers, indicating a clear road. "Let's rattle 'em," I grinned, and lifted the long, tubular regulator another inch or more up the boiler face. Sparks were flying from our dustbin-shaped chimney as our Q1 charged through the centre road at Eastleigh station. A swift glance at the overhead gantry at the platform end; the two signals proclaimed "All Clear" and the fireman bent to his task again. Incandescent white light reflected from the windows of Eastleigh West signal box as the engine and train roared past and on into the night. The next signal was now just a mere mile and a half away, and approaching fast. The fireman lifted his eyes from the firebox glare, and as they adjusted to the darkness, he spotted the Allbrook signal at "Danger". "On!" he screamed, "On!". Just for a moment I was unprepared, and did not comprehend, but perhaps sensing a collision, I moved the vacuum handle to the full application position, and brake blocks leapt onto wheels with a slam.

With the 'loose-coupleds' behind us, the brakes didn't have much immediate effect of course, but once the heavy engine and tender were under control, their combined weight aided by the up grade of the line quickly slowed the sixty wagons. Even so, the poor Guard would have had little time to take evasive action as each four-wheeler slammed into the buffers of its predecessor.

Attempting to see what lay ahead, my fireman and I stared fearfully from the footplate. Out of the darkness came a lone figure dressed in Guard's uniform, with its silver buttons glinting with the light of our fire. Swung slowly from side to side in his right hand was an oil lamp, its "Red" side towards us.

From the cabside I shouted,"What the hell's going on then?" as the offender started up the steps. "I got left behind by the Feltham up in front of you", came the reply. "I got the signalman to put the 'stick' "On" so you could give me a lift to Wallers Ash to pick up my train."

"You did what?," I screamed. "What do you think that did to my blood pressure? And above all, what do you

think its done to the poor sod in the van at the back? For all we know he's stretched out on the floor with his head bashed in! Get back and see if he's okay, and if he is, give us a "Green" light, and we'll get on with running this train!"

Muttering unavailing regrets, the erring Guard stumbled away along the ballast towards the Guards Van. The Q1 had been quietly simmering away up to this point, but the bright fire, coupled with the fact that the steam-chest no longer drew on boiler pressure, caused the safety valves to lift. With a roar, two solid jets of steam rose to the black night sky. A few moments passed, then a jade-green jewel of light was held high in the 'right away' position.

"That's it then," I said, and lifted the steam reverser to full forward and opened the regulator. The big 'Bulleid' eased forward, slack was taken up, and soon we were sailing along at the speed we had reached before the unfortunate stop.

"Nasty business that," I said after a while. "I only hope old Lucas is allright." The fireman nodded in agreement as our Q1 blasted on towards Winchester before I slowed again as requested 20 minutes later at Wallers Ash.

After a brief pause, another green light confirmed old Lucas was indeed still in the land of the living, and we stormed away once more exchanging rude gestures with the crew of the delayed 'Feltham' simmering quietly in the loop alongside. Our own destination was the yard at Basingstoke, and all was well as we progressed on through Micheldever, and up over the summit at Lichfield Tunnel

The hard work was done now, and the ever-efficient fireman had kept the boiler level low, so that the constant feeding of cold water kept steam pressure down and prevented constant lifting of the safety valves. The 'Charlies' were noted for their strong pulling capabilities, but as Mr. Bulleid found out in his earlier trials, the lightness of his Austerity Loco didn't make for the best of braking equipment. After the tunnel had been negotiated, the long run down into Basingstoke, via Worting flyover, always had to be treated with respect, or else a loose-fitted train of perhaps some 700 tons, with just the engine brake and guards van to assist, could be something of an embarrassment.

Via the engineman's 'grapevine', the 'Charlies' lack of stopping power was known far and wide, so the 2.02 a.m. from Bevois Park was eased very gently down into the Up Yard at Basingstoke. We ground gingerly to a halt at the oil-lit "DO NOT PROCEED WITHOUT SHUNTER'S PERMISSION" shunt board, although that night the said shunters didn't seem very keen to leave the warmth of their coal stove in the cabin!

Our Q1 stood quietly for a moment, but the fireman wasn't resting on his laurels. Opening the two steel doors, he hurled the firing shovel up into the tender coal hopper.

His task now was to throw a fresh supply of coal forward to use on the next lap of the journey, which with extra attachments to the train, would later go forward to Feltham Yard.

While this was going on, the Guard for whom everyone was so concerned, arrived at my side of the loco. The peak of his cap was pushed back, revealing the most prodigious lump - the size of an egg - on his head. "Are you O.K.?" I enquired, "I thought you might be dead." The unfortunate Guard replied, "I was pretty lucky. I was sitting down attending to the stove, when I heard them 'coming in'. I still got thrown across the van, and thumped my head on the side of the seat."

"You can blame your mate for that," I commented,

"Some blokes haven't got the sense they were born with. Take care of that head, and make sure you report it before you sign off..." Further conversation being impossible as once again the safety valves had started to lift. As the shunter arrived with the lamp and pole to start re-marshalling the train, our 'Charlie' stormed away up the yard with the first portion to be shunted, those unique beats "Shuff, shutting" away into the rain, which had by now, started to fall.

So was completed another chapter in the story of Q1 loco operations. 'Ugly ducklings' they perhaps were, but always hard workers, and although derided in many quarters, they are now remembered with affection by many an aged fireman.

C11 amidst the fug of a busy running shed - Guildford in late 1948. Built at Brighton, this particular engine was first allocated to Eastleigh but was later sent to Feltham, where it was destined to spend most of its working life. It was also unique in having a small 's' prefix added to the original C11 number between January 1948 and December 1950.

Tony Sedgwick

Brand new at Brighton in early 1942 and with the number attached on a riveted plate; this was removed before entering service. Trial running commenced in March from Brighton to either Worthing or Three Bridges, the more usual location for such trips, Eastbourne, at the time off-limits due to recent attention from enemy aircraft. Each engine built at the former LBSCR works followed a similar pattern for approximately two weeks before being despatched to its allocated depot.

Chapter 3

CONSTRUCTION AND DETAILS

All forty members of the class were built in 1942 in three batches, C1 - C16 at Brighton, C17- C36 at Ashford, and finally C37 - C40 also at Brighton. Interestingly, the 1946 Southern Railway building programme included provision for a further twenty 0-6-0s and some material was in fact ordered. However further engines of the type were destined to appear. All the boilers were built at Eastleigh, together with a further five spares also from Eastleigh in 1949. Unlike the fireboxes on his Pacific type, Bulleid's Q1 firebox was made of copper.

Wheelsets ready for the first of the class at Brighton. As with the Pacifics, the wheels were of cast steel and of the double-disc type, so affording greater support for the tyre. The result was a wheel which was destined to give excellent service although more noise was created at speed compared with conventional spokes.

Boiler and frames ready to be married. At the front of the engine can be seen the space for the overhead outside admission piston vales, which were operated through rocker shafts off two sets of Stephenson link motion. Some suggestion has been made that Bulleid would have used an oil-bath for the class if this could have been arranged and it is believed that it was only the urgent need for new locomotives at the time that precluded further work in this area.

Fitting out for No. C1. In the top view the two clack valves for the injectors are visible whilst an interesting feature of the design was the provision of the blower within the exhaust cavity, which, if operated by the driver as the regulator was shut, prevented the formation of a vacuum and the drawing of ash into the valves. In the lower view the formers for the lagging are shown to advantage, with the locomotive almost totally complete.

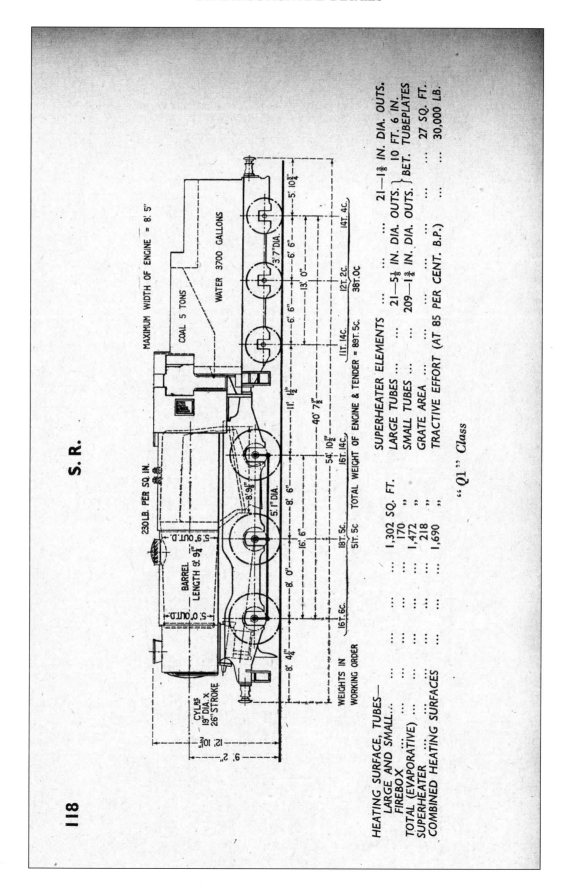

S. R.

118

CYL.S 19" DIA. X 26" STROKE

5' 0" OUT.D.

BARREL LENGTH 9' 9¼"

5' 9" OUT.D.

230LB. PER SQ. IN.

MAXIMUM WIDTH OF ENGINE = 8' 5"

COAL 5 TONS

WATER 3700 GALLONS

3' 7" DIA.

8' 9" DIA.

5.1" DIA.

8' 0" — 16' 6" — 8' 6" — 11' 1½" — 6' 6" — 13' 0" — 6' 6"

54' 10½"

40' 7½"

5' 10¾"

8' 4¼"

12' 10⅝"

9' 2"

WEIGHTS IN WORKING ORDER	16T.6c.	18T.5c.	5T. 5c	16T.14c.	11T.14c.	12T.2c.	14T. 4C.

TOTAL WEIGHT OF ENGINE & TENDER = 89T.5c. 38T.0C.

HEATING SURFACE, TUBES—				
LARGE AND SMALL...	...	...	...	1,302 SQ. FT.
FIREBOX ...	...	...	...	170 "
TOTAL (EVAPORATIVE) ...	...	...	...	1,472 "
SUPERHEATER ...	...	...	...	218 "
COMBINED HEATING SURFACES	...	...	...	1,690 "

SUPERHEATER ELEMENTS	...	...	...	21—1⅜ IN. DIA. OUTS.
LARGE TUBES ...	...	...	21—5⅛ IN. DIA. OUTS.	10 FT. 6 IN.
SMALL TUBES ...	...	...	209—1⅜ IN. DIA. OUTS.	} BET. TUBEPLATES
GRATE AREA ...	...	...	...	27 SQ. FT.
TRACTIVE EFFORT (AT 85 PER CENT. B.P.)	...	...	30,000 LB.

" Q1 " Class

19

Left - Mechanical lubricators to feed steamchests and cylinders were fitted from August 1942 commencing with C29. A further 15 members were similarly fitted later.

Above - Steam sanding was supplied with the container for the trailing coupled wheels located within the cab. Larger sand boxes were fitted to several of the class at Eastleigh in later years.

Tom Middlemas Collec.

Lower - With 3,700 gallons water capacity the tender could also carry 5 tons of coal. The tender was probably the poorest feature of the design and many suffered badly from leakage and corrosion.
David Lawrence / Hugh Davies 4665

Chapter 4

LIFE AND TIMES OF THE Q1 CLASS

After the introduction of the first of the class in 1942, C1 was set the task of taking a 1000-ton train from Woking up the gently rising grade to Basingstoke, a distance of some 24 miles. This it achieved without difficulty in 58 minutes, some 8 minutes less than the existing schedule for an 800 ton train over the same route. The standard was then set for the use of the class on heavy war-time traffic, in direct consequence of which C11- C20 were allocated new to Eastleigh to replace Maunsell 'Q' class engines.

Others of the type were sent new to various depots on the Eastern and Central Sections, with a number also concentrated at Feltham which depot supplied locomotives for the important cross-London freight traffic to Acton on the GW, Willesden on the LMS, and Fern Park (Hornsby) on the LNER.

There was also one regular turn from Redbridge (near Southampton) to Exmouth Junction, with the engine used then stabled overnight before returning east. Exmouth Junction though would sometimes 'borrow' it for other work, and in this way a Q1 was a regular visitor on the pick-up goods to Templecombe and also Okehampton. It is not thought members of the class ever ventured further west over the 'Withered Arm', whilst in practice most of the class were to seen east of Salisbury.

Guildford was also unique in that it had at some time seen every member of class allocated or on loan to the shed.

With peacetime restored there was no need to provide power for troop and Government specials, and in consequence the engines settled down to a fairly mundane existence of freight, engineers' and occasional empty stock workings. There were also though some regular passenger turns as well, notably on the Guildford to Horsham line and also to Tonbridge and Reading.

At peak periods there was also the occasional need for troop specials to and from Aldershot, whilst they were also used on summer Saturday extras when no other locomotive was available. But the black sooty form of the class was still most common on the cross London freight workings.

Throughout the twenty plus years of their existence they became part of the Southern scene in a way that no one could perhaps have envisaged back in 1942, and a valuable addition to the stud of motive power available to the operating department.

27 October 1945, and an extremely grimy and unidentified member of the class stands at Bournemouth Central apparently having arrived with a passenger working from Weymouth. This may well have been one of the earliest regular passenger workings of the class in the area. Alongside is another Bulleid creation, 21C15, as yet un-named, but later to become 'Rotterdam Lloyd'.

G.O. Pearce

Left - An unusual combination of a Q1 and a Merchant Navy. The location is not recorded, despite the obvious presence of the station in the background. Assisting a failing engine, or avoiding light engine working? The permutations are endless.
Tom Middlemas Collec.

Below - 33023 at the head of former LMS stock on the Saturdays only train from the LMR to Bournemouth via the Salisbury and Fordingbridge line. 23 July 1960. At the time this was an Eastleigh-based engine and indeed had been so allocated for the previous twelve years. Although such a working over this particular route would not require any great speed, the class were well able to reach speeds in excess of 60 mph when required although the noise the crew was subjected to was considerable. Running in reverse was best described as 'lively', and had earlier given rise to complaints by the crews, although after Bulleid travelled especially on one of the class under these conditions such grumbles decreased.
A. Gosling

Right - Feltham shed, 1 September 1958. 33026 and 30509 at rest. The Q1 had been transferred to this depot from Tonbridge in September 1953, and would remain here for nearly all its remaining life.

Below - A heavy load for an unidentified member of the class. The restricted braking power of the engines was later countered by the provision of either additional brake vans or a 'vacuum fitted head' when required.
R. Stumpf Collec.

33010 in 1963 alongside what may well be the coaling stage at Weymouth. There is evidence of a slight leak from the steam reverser, whilst the equipment for the AWS is visible on the framing underneath the cab. The nickname 'Austerities' apparently originated from the Daily Express, and was of course later applied to a number of other contemporary steam types. Despite the need for speed in design, care taken had ensured the steam passages were well laid out and this, allied to a multiple-jet blastpipe, contributed to free running. Aside from having a similar size firebox to the 'Lord Nelson' class, the design also used a standard Drummond steam reverser, and the braking was straight from the Maunsell 'Q' class - a modification to improve the braking performance was never implemented. Interestingly, the cab roof always appeared foreshortened, and when questioned about this the draughtsman responsible is reported to have commented that he, "...had reached the edge of the paper." The mechanical lubricator fitted replaced the original displacement lubricators on several of the class, whilst the boiler pressure was set at 230 psi rather than the 220 psi that had originally been intended. The squared-off lower section of the casing afforded some form of splasher, but did not prevent rain water being thrown up and impairing the driver's vision. Despite increasing the thickness of the material used for the smokebox in later years, the original shape was retained, although all of the class (with the possible exception of 33028), had been fitted with Swindon pattern spark arresters by April 1963. All also had water treatment, whilst a number were also fitted with AWS to some degree. Tender difficulties have been referred to previously; the actual tender frames are believed to have all been built at Ashford and the bodies fitted at Lancing. With the exception of the frames then, the actual erection of the locomotives at either Brighton or Ashford was being mainly the assembly of various parts brought together. Scheduled mileage between heavy overhauls was set at 70,000 miles, although a number of the class regularly exceeded this figure. The average mileage per year being slightly over 20,000, or something like 384 per week.

J. H. Aston

24

Chapter 5

THE LOCOMOTIVES - AN INDIVIDUAL RECORD

Note: Information for the individual records has been compiled from a variety of sources, individual locomotive cards held at the National Railway Museum, various ABC's, published works and sundry observations. Not surprisingly there are occasionally some discrepancies. The information given though is as accurate as it has been possible to obtain. Where obvious discrepancies appear these are highlighted.

C1 / 33001

The prototype of the class was built at Brighton and outshopped on 2 March 1942.

Sheds	
First shed	Guildford
May 1959	Tonbridge
June 1959	Feltham
May 1961	Tonbridge
September 1963	Guildford

Repairs and Works Visits

Regrettably the only missing record for any of the class is that for 33001. No details of repairs etc can then therefore be given.

Withdrawn June 1964 but preserved for the National Collection. Stored for many years at the old Pullman car depot at Brighton before being loaned to the Bulleid Society by the National Railway Museum and currently on the Bluebell Railway.

The first of the class, C1, in late Southern Railway days and already modified with smokebox handrails and what appear to be additional oil pipes.
R. M. Casserley

C2 / 33002

Built at Brighton and outshopped in May 1942.

Sheds	
First shed	Guildford
February 1953	Faversham
March 1953	Guildford
May / June 1959	Tonbridge
January 1961	Ramsgate

Tender No.	
As built	3142
23/10/1944	3180
31/3/1946	3146 exchanged
	at Guildford
31/10/46	3169 where ?

Repairs and Works visits	Works / Depot	Type of Repair	Returned to service	Mileage since last general repair
22/10/1942	Eastleigh	B	5/11/1942	6132
23/10/1944	Guildford	C	21/11/1944	
10/8/1945	Nine Elms	C	31/3/1946?	
30/11/1953	Ashford	L/Int	19/12/1953	50003
31/3/1955	Guildford	L/Cas	23/4/1955	
20/1/1956	Ashford	Gen	17/2/1956	94097
1/3/1957	Guildford	L/Cas	21/3/1957	24418
27/12/1957	Guildford	L/Cas	28/12/1957	45618
27/3/1958	Ashford	L/Int	19/4/1958	52096
25/8/1960	Ashford	Gen	15/10/1960	110089
12/2/1962	Bricklayers Arms	N/C	13/2/1962	
24/9/1962	Eastleigh	L/Cas	13/10/1962	40438

Boiler Number	
As built	1117
Nov 1953	1135
January 1956	1133
August 1960	1114

Modifications include WR type spark arrestor, AWS, water treatment complete, protector glasses to side of cab, tender handrails and pipes lagged.

Withdrawn 7 July 1963,
sold 7 March 1964.

33002 at Norwood on 12 September 1952 and carrying the headcode for what was probably a New Cross working. Interestingly the scheduled mileage for the class between general repairs was set at 70000 miles. 33002 is one of several that certainly exceeded this figure.

Tony Sedgwick

C3 / 33003

Built at Brighton and outshopped in May 1942. After trails recorded as at work on 5 June 1942.

Sheds	
First shed	Guildford
May / June 1959	Tonbridge
Jan 1961	Feltham

Tender No.	
As built	3143
21/8/1944	3147

Boiler No.	
As built	1119
October 1946	1122
December 1950	1120
May 1955	1126
January 1959	1139

Repairs and Works visits	Works / Depot	Type of Repair	Returned to service	Mileage since last general repair
20/6/1942	Eastleigh	D	22/6/1942	22
27/6/1942	Eastleigh	D	29/6/1942	22
7/12/1942	Eastleigh	D	17/12/1942	11019
10/11/1943	Eastleigh	D	17/11/1943	38061
21/8/1944	Eastleigh	C	16/9/1944	43101
7/4/1945	Guildford	C	22/5/1945	
9/11/1945	Nine Elms	C	12/11/1945	
5/10/1946	Ashford	D	15/11/1946	104487
13/11/1947	Ashford	D	16/1/1948	14122
22/3/1949	Nine Elms	N/C	22/3/1949	
18/11/1949	Guildford		13/12/1949	
6/12/1950	Ashford	Gen	5/1/1951	88383
22/4/1953	Ashford	H/Int	8/5/1953	
11/5/1955	Ashford	Gen	27/5/1955	
8/3/1957	Ashford	H/Int	31/3/1957	
6/1/1959	Ashford	Gen	30/1/1959	93398
9/2/1961	Ashford	H/Int	10/3/1961	43346
20/10/1961	Eastleigh	H/Cas	1/11/1961	55582

Engine involved in tests with varying size front and back rings in 1946.

Withdrawn 14 June 1964.

The products of Drummond and Bulleid side by side at Feltham. Left is H16 No. 30519 and to the right a 700 class 30326. As mentioned above this engine was the subject of a test in 1946 pertaining to ring sizes. Whether this related to piston or valve rings is not reported, likewise whether or not this was a temporary affair.

Tony Sedgwick

C4 / 33004

Built at Brighton and outshopped on 8 June 1942.

Sheds

First shed	Guildford
February 1953	Faversham
May 1959	Tonbridge
January 1961	Feltham
September 1963	Three Bridges
December 1963	Guildford

Tender No.

As built	3149
28/5/1945	3141

Boiler No.

As built	1122
15/10/1946	1119
8/10/1953	1130
19/11/1957	1117

Repairs and Works visits	Works / Depot	Type of Repair	Returned to service	Mileage since last general repair
6/10/1942	Eastleigh	D	10/10/1940	4868
22/11/1943	Eastleigh	D	20/12/1943	36289
11/9/1944	Guildford	C	3/10/1944	
9/2/1945	Nine Elms	C	10/2/1945	
2/4/1945	Guildford	C	18/5/1945	
28/5/1945	Nine Elms	C	29/5/1945	
26/7/1945	Nine Elms	C	26/7/1945	
29/12/1945	Nine Elms	C	2/1/1946	
15/1/1946	Guildford	C	6/2/1946	
15/10/1946	Ashford	A	23/11/1946	97279
27/10/1947	Nine Elms		29/10/1947	
13/10/1948	Ashford	Int?	30/10/1948	43248
9/1/1949	Nine Elms		9/1/1949	
1/3/1949	Guildford		16/3/1949	
6/10/1949	Ashford	H/Int	18/11/1949	63205
15/11/1950	Guildford		18/12/1950	
1/1/1952	Ashford	L/Int	1/2/1952	120743
7/2/1952	Ashford	Defect	8/2/1952	
8/10/1953	Ashford	Gen	24/10/1953	161256
21/10/1954	Guildford		12/11/1954	
10/5/1955	Ashford	L/Cas	27/5/1955	43154
30/11/1955	Ashford	L/Cas	17/12/1955	55174
12/7/1956	Ashford	H/Int	18/8/1956	70887
18/12/1956	Ashford	N/C	28/12/1956	143114
19/11/1957	Ashford	Gen	14/12/1957	101632
3/4/1959	Ashford	L/Cas	18/4/1959	34103
12/7/1960	Ashford	L/Int	6/8/1960	63110
28/8/1962	Eastleigh	H/Int	22/9/1962	110488
29/5/1963	Eastleigh	N/C	5/9/1963	117077

Modifications reported include the fitting of a WR type spark arrester, pipes lagged, safety links, AWS, and water treatment completed.

The engine was also subject to test No. 1957 involving fitting of a 'Firthag' steel chimney and ashpan at Ashford on 18 November 1949.

Withdrawn 3 January 1965.

Another member of the type achieving a very high mileage between repairs was 33004 seen here running west past Alderbury Junction and bound for Salisbury but definitely displaying a confusing head-code! It had received its BR number in October 1948
R. Blencowe Collec.

C5 / 33005

Built at Brighton and outshopped in June 1942.

Repairs and Works visits	Works / Depot	Type of Repair	Returned to service	Mileage since last general repair
5/9/1942	Eastleigh	B	7/9/1942	2881
18/12/1942	Eastleigh	B	30/12/1942	10521
10/8/1943	Eastleigh	B	18/8/1943	28806
19/2/1944	Guildford	C	27/3/1944	46527
21/2/1945	Nine Elms	C	21/2/1945	

Sheds	
First shed	Guildford
February 1953	Ashford
March 1953	Faversham
April 1953	Guildford

Tender No.	
As built	?
By 5/9/1942	3145
21/2/1945	3153
15/5/1946	3168 or 3180 exchanged at Guildford.

Boiler Number	
As built	1123

Note: The engine record card held at the National Railway Museum is clearly incomplete as no entries are recorded after 1945.

Withdrawn June 1963

33005 on the 5.05 pm Alton to Woking pick-up goods, Monday 11 April 1960. Bryan Kimber

C6 / 33006

Built at Brighton and outshopped on
24 June 1942.

Sheds

First shed	Guildford
January 1950	Feltham
September 1963	?
June 1964	Feltham
November 1964	Guildford
June 1965	Nine Elms
October 1965	Guildford

Tender No.

As built	3144
29/9/1944	3169
5/3/1945	3168

Boiler No.

As built	1132
5/7/1947	1137
21/3/1950	1138
23/4/1954	1119
3/6/1960	1176

Repairs and Works visits	Works / Depot	Type of Repair	Returned to service	Mileage since last general repair
8/10/1942	Eastleigh	D	14/10/1942	5673
28/5/1943	Eastleigh	D	31/5/1943	25000
29/9/1944	Guildford	C	19/10/1944	
4/7/1945	Nine Elms	C	4/7/1945	
25/9/1944	Guildford		19/10/1944	
5/3/1945	Ashford	C	6/4/1945	64435
4/7/1945	Nine Elms		4/7/1945	
28/9/1945	Guildford	C	7/1/1946	
25/5/1946	Ashford	C	22/6/1946	80265
20/11/1946	Nine Elms	C	20/11/1946	
5/7/1947	Ashford	A	16/8/1947	100715
16/2/1948	Nine Elms		16/2/1948	
29/4/1948	Nine Elms	D	1/5/1948	12175
31/3/1950	Nine Elms	H/Cas	14/4/1950	58294
3/3/1952	Ashford	H/Int	21/3/1952	101106
26/3/1952	Ashford	Defect	28/3/1952	
23/4/1954	Ashford	Gen	15/5/1954	140248
12/12/1955	Ashford	U/C	29/12/1955	38118
12/6/1956	Ashford	H/Int	29/6/1956	45977
14/3/1958	Ashford	H/Int	12/4/1958	37669
3/6/1960	Ashford	Gen	9/7/1960	152739
23/3/1962?	Bricklayers Arms	N/C	21/3/1962	
16/2/1963	Eastleigh	L/Int	16/2/1963	47657

Withdrawn 9 January 1966.

Does Q1 + Q1 = Q2? 33006 and 33011 double head a troop special just west of Pirbright Junction and probably bound for either Tidworth or Bulford. The use of double heading was unusual but was probably due to a need to run the train to a fast schedule. Arthur Tayler

33007 leaving Southampton Central on 19 July 1958 and heading towards Bournemouth and Weymouth with a special working from the Eastern Region. Throughout the 1950's this was a Feltham based machine and had no doubt been 'borrowed' for this particular train.

R. Blencowe Collec.

C7 / 33007

Built at Brighton and outshopped on 6 July 1942.

Modifications including pipes lagged, safety links, spark arrestor, water treatment, AWS and modified gangway doors.

Sheds

First shed	Guildford
February 1950	Feltham
February 1953	Hither Green
April 1953	Feltham

Tender No.

As built	3146
20/7/1944	3162
24/8/1953	3143
20/4/1957	3156

Boiler Number

As built	1127
By June 1945	1141
7/2/1947	1127
8/5/1950	1132
24/8/1953	1141
13/3/1957	1150

Repairs and Works visits	Works / Depot	Type of Repair	Returned to service	Mileage since last general repair
20/7/1944	Ashford	C	9/9/1944	43327
3/6/1945	Guildford	C	11/7/1945	
24/11/1945	Nine Elms	C	26/11/1945	
7/2/1947	Ashford	A	15/3/1947	104970
2/12/1947	Nine Elms		3/12/1947	
7/3/1949	Guildford		25/3/1949	
8/5/1950	Ashford	A	2/6/1950	71605
30/5/1952	Ashford	L/Int	20/6/1950	38073
3/7/1952	Ashford	Defect		
16/7/1952	Ashford	Defect	18/7/1952	
23/7/1952	Ashford	Defect	1/8/1952	
24/8/1952	Ashford	Gen	12/9/1953	60433
23/9/1953	Ashford	N/C	25/9/1953	
1/6/1954	Guildford	N/C	4/6/1954	16621
22/4/1955	Ashford	L/Cas	12/5/1955	
1/12/1955	Ashford	L/Cas	23/12/1955	47254
13/3/1957	Ashford	Gen	6/4/1957	71825
20/4/1957	Ashford	L/Int	9/5/1959	52335
21/4/1961	Ashford	H/Int	13/5/1961	1010674
4/4/1963	Eastleigh	L/Cas	27/4/1963	138449

Withdrawn 1 February 1964.

C8 / 33008

Built at Brighton and outshopped in July 1942.

Sheds	
First shed	Guildford
December 1948	Feltham

Tender No.	
As built	3167

Repairs and Works visits	Works / Depot	Type of Repair	Returned to service	Mileage since last general repair
9/3/1953	Ashford	Gen		
11/3/1955	Ashford	H/Int		
23/10/1956	Ashford	H/Int		
9/10/1958	Ashford	Gen		
30/8/1960	Guildford	L/GRS?		
20/6/1961	Ashford	H/Int		

Modifications known of were, mechanical lubricator in November 1956, modified gangway doors, pipes lagged and footplate glass on cab(?).

Withdrawn August 1963.

33008, another member of the type where the surviving records are incomplete. Although undated, the photograph was taken sometime after 1955 and aside from the revised BR emblem on the tender, electrification flashes have appeared together with additional cabside embellishments.

33009 at rest between duties. This engine was only part-fitted with AWS - in which respect is not reported, but it did have a WR-type spark arrester, water treatment and lagged pipes. All these items added or amended on unrecorded dates. 33009 was the last to receive a general repair, at late as January / February 1963. It was the practice after that time to keep the engines running until a major defect developed and most were withdrawn in what was a run-down poor condition.

Tony Sedgwick

C9 / 33009

Built at Brighton and outshopped on 31 July 1942.

Sheds

First shed	Guildford
April 1948	Feltham
February 1953	Hither Green
September 1964	Guildford
June 1965	Nine Elms

Tender No.

As built	3117
13/1/1945	3143
13/5/1952	3162

Boiler Number

As built	1126
6/4/1950	1174
24/5/1956	1131
21/1/1963	1162

Repairs and Works visits	Works / Depot	Type of Repair	Returned to service	Mileage since last general repair
19/10/1942	Eastleigh	D	20/10/1942	
6/4/1944	Ashford	C	6/5/1944	45174
27/11/1944	Guildford		22/12/1944	
4/10/1945	Guildford	C	26/10/1945	
20/9/1946	Ashford	A	19/10/1946	100273
13/10/1947	Nine Elms		17/10/1947	
21/10/1948	Nine Elms		28/10/1948	39723
6/4/1950	Ashford	A	12/5/1950	69285
13/5/1952	Ashford	H/Int	11/7/1952	45654
23/7/1952	Ashford	Defect	24/7/1952	
20/5/1954	Ashford	H/Int	5/6/1954	90637
24/5/1956	Ashford	Gen	15/6/1956	136588
3/3/1958	Ashford	H/Int	21/3/1958	42273
7/4/1960	?		7/5/1960	
5/4/1962	Bricklayers Arms	N/C	6/4/1962	
21/1/1963	Eastleigh	Gen	2/3/1963	136684

A Molyneaux

33021 on a down freight just south of Shawford, 25 May 1960.

Above: 33006 at Guildford, 12 June 1965. At the time one of only six members of the class still active.

Keith Robertson Collec.

Lower: Guildford in September 1965 and by now with just four engines in service.

Colour Rail

J.E. Bell

33039 running round at Bulford Camp with the special LCGB 'Hampshire Venturer', 10 March 1963.

Above: Passenger duty at Sittingbourne and with definite evidence of previous hard work showing.   *Colour Rail*

Lower: 33008 on Parkstone bank with a Poole to Bournemouth freight in April 1961.   *Colour Rail*

C10 / 33010

Built at Brighton and outshopped on
21 August 1942.

Sheds

First shed	Guildford
April 1948	Feltham

Tender No.

As built	3153
10/11/1943	3166
6/4/1945	3168
9/10/1946	3153
24/10/1950	3175

Boiler Number

As built	1134
9/10/1946	1142
24/10/1950	1121
24/1/1955	1153
2/7/1959	1147

Repairs and Works visits	Works / Depot	Type of Repair	Returned to service	Mileage since last general repair
23/10/1942	Ashford	D	9/11/1942	3722
10/11/1943	Eastleigh	D	19/11/1943	31884
14/1/1944	Guildford	C	18/2/1944	34368
24/3/1944	Eastleigh	C	1/4/1944	37449
28/4/1944	Ashford	C	10/6/1944	39900
6/4/1945	Nine Elms	C	6/4/1945	68845
24/6/1945	Nine Elms	C	24/6/1945	72480
11/11/1945	Guildford	C	19/11/1945	
1/2/1946	Eastleigh	C	9/2/1946	82372
20/7/1946	Nine Elms		21/7/1946	
9/10/1946	Ashford	A	16/11/1946	96685
27/2/1948	Nine Elms	D	8/3/1948	
	Nine Elms		15/4/1948	32177
2/11/1949	Eastleigh	L/Int	18/11/1949	60542
	Nine Elms		11/5/1949	50053
2/11/1949	Eastleigh	L/Int	23/11/1949	
24/10/1950	Ashford	H/Cas	22/11/1950	79480
13/10/1952	Ashford	H/Int	31/10/1952	
14/11/1952	Ashford	Defect	19/11/1952	
14/5/1953	Feltham		16/6/1953	
24/1/1955	Ashford	Gen	14/2/1955	171192
3/8/1956	Guildford	L/Cas	25/8/1945	32022
15/5/1957	Ashford	H/Int	1/6/1957	47468
2/7/1959	Ashford	Gen	25/7/1959	99657
29/3/1960	Ashford	L/Cas	16/4/1960	17334
10/8/1961	Eastleigh	H/Int	9/9/1961	47563
21/11/1962	Eastleigh	L/Cas	8/12/1962	68317

Withdrawn January 1964

C11 / 33011

Outshopped from
Brighton 09/42

In later years water
treatment added, pipes
lagged, handrails
modified and protector
glasses fitted.

Sheds

First shed	Eastleigh
May 1947	Basingstoke
April 1948	Feltham
February 1953	Hither Green
April 1953	Feltham

Repairs and Works visits	Works / Depot	Type of Repair	Returned to service	Mileage since last general repair
3722 7/7/1953	Ashford	Gen	25/7/1953	
17/3/1955	Ashford	H/Int	6/4/1955	
7/11/1956	Ashford	L/Cas	21/11/1956	
30/5/1957	Ashford	L/Int	22/6/1957	
3/7/1959	Ashford	Gen	25/7/1959	
21/7/1961	Ashford	H/Int	2/9/1961	

Withdrawn 26 September 1965, reported as
scrapped at Eastleigh, 19 October 1963.

Above: C10 - later 33010, at Guildford in 1947. This particular engine was renumbered by BR in November 1949 and is likely to have achieved the highest mileage of any of the type between general repairs. A staggering 171,192 miles.

Tony Sedgwick

Below: C11 (renumbered 33011 in December 1950), at its first home depot of Eastleigh. The grime which was so typical of the class is apparent and was typical of many designated freight engines. The limited cleaning resources available being restricted to the passenger types.

W. Gilburt

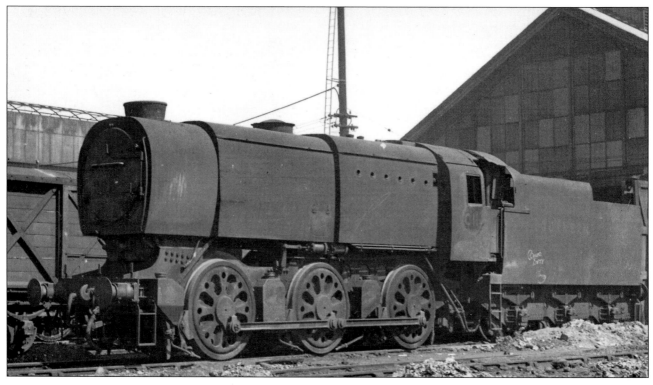

A travel stained C12 outside Feltham depot in February 1949 and with obvious evidence of priming. The BR number was applied to this engine in January 1950.

C.H.S. Owen

C12 / 33012

Built at Brighton and outshopped in September 1942.

Sheds	
First shed	Eastleigh
March 1944	Fratton
July 1947	Guildford
April 1948	Feltham
September 1964	Guildford

Tender No.	
As built	3152

Boiler Number	
As built	1138
29/12/1949	1153
1/6/54	1124

Repairs and Works visits	Works / Depot	Type of Repair	Returned to service	Mileage since last general repair
17/11/1942	Eastleigh	D	2/12/1942	689
4/6/1943	Eastleigh	D	12/6/1943	11941
27/10/1943	Eastleigh	D	29/10/1943	22822
7/6/1944	Eastleigh	C	16/6/1944	35684
9/2/1945	Eastleigh Shed	C	22/3/1945	40127
21/5/1946	Eastleigh	C	15/6/1946	78162
17/12/1946	Eastleigh	C	4/1/1947	87574
19/2/1947	Eastleigh	C	1/3/1947	88120
17/8/1947	Eastleigh	C	24/9/1947	
31/12/1947	Ashford	C	7/2/1948	102971
29/12/1949	Ashford	A	27/1/1950	143076
14/11/1951	Ashford	H/Int	14/12/1951	35779
1/6/1954	Ashford	Gen	3/7/1954	88537
5/11/1954	Ashford	H/Cas	20/11/1954	
9/10/1956	Ashford	L/Int	7/10/1956	47942
20/3/1957	Ashford	Cas	13/4/1957	55724
31/10/1958	Ashford	?	22/11/1958	94324
4/7/1960	Ashford	Gen	30/7/1960	129519
30/11/1962	Eastleigh	H/Int	5/1/1963	49480

This engine was fitted with 3" Ross safety valves with stainless steel valve seats at Ashford on 27 January 1950.

Withdrawn 22 November 1964.

Fresh from overhaul at Ashford, 33013 waits a return to its home depot of Feltham on 9 July 1950 This engine was the subject of a test involving the fitting of mechanical lubricators to the axle-boxes on 14 September 1946. Official records also state that it was not renumbered until August 1950.

W. Gilburt

C13 / 33013

Built at Brighton and outshopped on 9 October 1942.

Sheds

First shed	Eastleigh
December 1947	Guildford
April 1948	Feltham

Tender No.

As built	3154
16/5/1960	3164

Boiler Number

As built	1140
25/5/1950	1176
16/5/1960	1145

Withdrawn 7 July 1963, sold 7 March 1964.

Repairs and Works visits	Works / Depot	Type of Repair	Returned to service	Mileage since last general repair
22/1/1943	Eastleigh	D	29/1/1943	4256
4/5/1943	Eastleigh	D	6/5/1943	
29/10/1943	Eastleigh	D	5/11/1943	24518
31/7/1943	Eastleigh	C	11/8/1943	43138
8/12/1944	Eastleigh	A	6/1/1945	48202
13/3/1946	Eastleigh	D	1/4/1946	72556
12/8/1946	Eastleigh	A	14/9/1946	78202
14/11/1947	Nine Elms		17/11/1947	
25/5/1950	Ashford	Gen	23/6/1950	77120
1/1/1952	Ashford	H/Int	29/1/1952	32587
6/2/1952	Ashford	Defect	11/2/1952	
13/2/1952	Ashford	Defect	15/2/1952	
13/2/1953	Feltham		28/3/1953	56080
25/11/1953	Ashford	L/Int	17/10/1953	71833
28/11/1955	?	Gen	17/12/1955	113174
9/12/1957	Ashford	L/Int	4/1/1958	45806
3/12/1958	Ashford	L/Cas	13/12/1958	67097
26/3/1959	Guildford	L/Cas	11/4/1959	
16/5/1960	Ashford	Gen	25/6/1960	46884
5/6/1962	Eastleigh	Non-class	9/6/1962	42315

Wearing a mixture of Southern and BR insignia, 33014 is posed outside Eastleigh Shed on 11 March 1950. The engine had reportedly been renumbered on 8 April 1949 and here is proof it may have taken longer to get around to the tender. The loco was also fitted with safety links, AWS and had lagged pipes, whilst Test No. 2062 of 2 November 1962 saw a Klinger drain cock fitted to the left hand water gauge only.

Tony Sedgwick

C14 / 33014

Built at Brighton and outshopped on 22 October 1942.

Sheds

First shed	Eastleigh
August 1950	Guildford
July 1951	Hither Green
May 1959	Tonbridge
January 1961	Nine Elms
December 1962	?
December 1963	Guildford

Tender No.

As built	3156
2/3/1944	3176
22/1/1946	3146

Boiler Number

As built	1142
3/10/1946	1134
8/12/1958	1142
23/11/1960	1127

Repairs and Works visits	Works / Depot	Type of Repair	Returned to service	Mileage since last general repair
17/6/1943	Eastleigh	D	24/6/1943	14387
	Eastleigh	D		19048
2/3/1944	Eastleigh	C	11/3/1944	31886
28/10/1944	Eastleigh	C	2/12/1944	49546
22/1/1946	Eastleigh	C	26/1/1946	70623
3/10/1946	Ashford	A	2/11/1946	82826
18/11/1947	Eastleigh	D	22/11/1947	22400
8/4/1949	Eastleigh	L/Cas	8/4/1949	47065
25/5/1950	Ashford	Gen	30/6/1950	69352
7/8/1951	Guildford		20/8/1951	28167
17/2/1953	Ashford	H/Int	6/3/1953	58161
30/7/1954	Ashford	H/Int	28/8/1954	91782
8/3/1955	Ashford	L/Cas	18/3/1955	105609
30/11/1955	Ashford	Gen	23/12/1955	123727
30/10/1957	Ashford	L/Int	16/11/1957	43136
8/12/1958	Ashford	L/Cas	3/1/1959	70417
30/6/1959	Ashford	H/Cas	18/7/1959	78354
10/12/1959	Ashford	N/C	31/12/1959	88717
23/11/1960	Ashford	Gen	30/12/1960	109434

Withdrawn in January 1964.

33015 running light engine through Woking and en-route to Guildford. Aside from the more usual additions of lagged pipes, AWS and projector glass fitted in the cab, this engine also had blowdown gear and silencer and a briquette tube feeder for the water softening equipment. It was reported also that the tender handrails had been renewed although no date is given. Withdrawn on 15 November 1964 it was cut up by contractors on 27 February 1965.

A. Gosling

C15 / 33015

Built at Brighton and outshopped on 6 November 1942.

Sheds	
First shed	Eastleigh
August 1950	Guildford
July 1951	Hither Green
June 1954	?
October 1954	Stewarts Lane
January 1955	Nine Elms
January 1961	Feltham
December 1962	?
December 1963	Guildford

Tender No.	
As built	3155
16/5/1944	3157

Boiler Number	
As built	1144
17/7/1952	1124
2/12/1953	1125
30/7/1958	1148
23/7/1962	1115

Repairs and Works visits	Works / Depot	Type of Repair	Returned to service	Mileage since last general repair
29/12/1942	Eastleigh	D	6/1/1943	299
10/4/1943	Eastleigh	C	23/4/1943	6400
16/5/1944	Fratton		19/6/1944	32097
8/8/1944	Eastleigh	C	22/8/1944	34922
11/4/1945	Eastleigh	D	28/4/1944	53231
8/1/1946	Eastleigh Shed	C	10/2/1946	70179
27/3/1946	Eastleigh	C	30/3/1946	81739
25/10/1946	Eastleigh	D	2/11/1946	
14/5/1947	Ashford	D	14/6/1947	90189
23/2/1950	Ashford	H/Int	23/3/1950	56437
29/9/1950	Ashford	H/Cas	3/11/1950	69370
17/7/1952	Ashford	Gen	7/8/1952	109877
2/12/1953	Ashford	Gen	31/12/1953	36799
8/5/1955	Nine Elms		17/6/1955	
5/7/1956	Ashford	L/Int	10/8/1956	57261
30/7/1958	Ashford	Gen	16/8/1958	47699
21/6/1961	Ashford	L/Cas	18/3/1961	42054
15/9/1961	Bricklayers Arms	N/C	19/9/1961	
23/7/1962	Eastleigh	Gen	1/9/1962	64342

33016 and 'U' class 2-6-0 31634 at Waterloo. Q1s were not a regular feature of the Waterloo scene and the reason for its appearance may well be pondered. The side protector glasses to the rear of the cab - compared with the cab view on page 8, are clearly displayed in this view although interestingly there is no official reference to them on the record cards for this engine.

A.C. Ingram

C16 / 33016

Built at Brighton and outshopped in November 1942.

Later reported as fitted with AWS, water treatment and pipes lagged.

Tests reported include:

No. 2005. Driving axleboxes. 18/5/1946.
    1934. Leading and trailing axleboxes. 18/5/1946.
    1977. Warm Gauge protection. 1948.
    2133. 3" diameter Ross safety valves. 24/3/1950.

New cylinders fitted. 18/5/46.

Repairs and Works visits	Works / Depot	Type of Repair	Returned to service	Mileage since last general repair
17/11/1942	Brighton	C	22/2/1943	
10/4/1943	Eastleigh	D	15/4/1943	
1/5/1943	Eastleigh	D	3/5/1943	
21/6/1943	Eastleigh	D	21/6/1943	
13/8/1943	Eastleigh	D	18/8/1943	10107
16/9/1943	Eastleigh	D	25/9/1943	13455
30/11/1944	Eastleigh	C	27/1/1945	43454
13/4/1945	Eastleigh	C	4/5/1945	47231
10/4/1946	Eastleigh	A	18/5/1946	46226
6/3/1947	Eastleigh	D	14/3/1967	17556
29/4/1952	Eastleigh	Weighing	29/4/1952	44611

Sheds	
First shed	Eastleigh
August 1950	Guildford
June 1951	Fratton
January 1952	Eastleigh
February 1953	Faversham
April 1954	Norwood Junction
October 1954	Feltham
December 1962	Three Bridges

Tender No.	
As built	3176
30/11/44	3156

Boiler Number	
As built	1146

Withdrawn August 1963.

C17, numerically the first of the Ashford built engines although not the first to be completed, and recorded at Eastleigh in June 1949. In common with a number of the class it was modified in later years with AWS equipment, spark arrester gear and had pipework lagged. Safety links were also fitted.

R. Blencowe Collec

C17 / 33017

Built at Ashford and outshopped in May 1942.

Sheds

First shed	Eastleigh
March 1943	Basingstoke
By May 1949	Eastleigh
April 1954	Brighton
October 1954	Stewarts Lane
January 1955	Nine Elms
January 1961	Feltham
December 1962	Three Bridges

Tender No.

As built	3155
17/9/1946	3165

Tests reported include:

No. 2048. Piston valves. 12/10/1946
    2038. Mech lubricator for axleboxes
        12/10/1948
    2133. Ross safety valves and seats fitted at
        Ashford on 30/12/1949.
New cylinders fitted 17/5/1947.

Withdrawn January 1964

Repairs and Works visits	Works / Depot	Type of Repair	Returned to service	Mileage since last general repair
15/8/1942	Eastleigh	D	18/8/1942	6004
8/1/1943	Eastleigh	D	16/1/1943	12967
2/10/1943	Eastleigh	D	8/10/1943	30320
16/8/1944	Eastleigh	C	26/8/1944	50199
17/9/1946	Eastleigh	A	12/10/1946	89082
8/4/1947	Eastleigh	B	17/5/1947	6343
20/10/1947	Eastleigh	C	25/10/1947	13801
21/11/1951	Eastleigh	L/Cas	28/11/1951	98309
19/12/1951	Eastleigh	N/C	27/12/1951	98309
2/1/1953	Ashford	H/Int	23/1/1953	
10/10/1955	Ashford	Gen	4/11/1955	
5/10/1956	Ashford	L/Cas	26/10/1956	
29/11/1957	Ashford	L/Int	21/12/1957	
25/3/1960	Ashford	Gen	30/4/1960	
28/8/1961	Eastleigh	L/Cas	30/9/1961	

Boiler Number

As built	1115

Proving its worth as a mixed traffic engine, although any attempt to run at speed could be exciting at the very least for the crew. 33018 is seen near Farnborough North heading for Ash on a special working and made up to at least a 10 coach train. Two tests are known of for this machine, a driving axlebox pump was fitted on 4 May 1946, and at the same time Firthag Steel heat resistant steel firebars. In all the cases of the tests mentioned there is no information as to whether the engines carried the same modifications throughout their lives. Notice also the smokebox handrails have reverted to a more normal type - see page 11.
Bob Barnard / Hugh Davies

C18 / 33018

Built at Ashford and outshopped 8 April 1942.

Sheds

First shed	Eastleigh
March 1944	Basingstoke
March 1953	Ramsgate
May 1953	Guildford
September 1953	Hither Green
April 1954	Norwood Junction
October 1954	Feltham
December 1962	Three Bridges
December 1963	Guildford
June 1965	Nine Elms

Tender No.

As built	3158

Boiler Number

As built	1116

Repairs and Works visits	Works / Depot	Type of Repair	Returned to service	Mileage since last general repair
18/6/1942	Ashford	D	19/6/1942	864
11/12/1942	Eastleigh	C	23/12/1942	12259
11/8/1943	Eastleigh	D	17/8/1943	30862
25/5/1944	Eastleigh	C	4/6/1944	53966
3/3/1945	Ashford	C	17/3/1945	67357
10/8/1945	Nine Elms	C	10/8/1945	73468
24/11/1945	Ashford		19/1/1946	83560
11/3/1946	Ashford	C	3/5/1946	2238
3/10/1946	Eastleigh	D	12/10/1946	7133
1/10/1947	Eastleigh Shed		11/11/1947	
18/5/1949	Ashford		18/6/1949	58242
19/9/1951	Ashford	1123	18/10/1951	104350
1/11/1951	Ashford		5/11/1951	
11/9/1953	Ashford	H/Int	3/10/1953	48685
12/5/1954	Ashford	L/Cas	12/6/1954	65297
4/1/1956	Ashford	Gen	28/1/1956	100890
30/1/1958	Ashford	L/Int	22/2/1958	47124
11/2/1960	Ashford	Gen	5/3/1960	88442
16/4/1962	Eastleigh	Non Class	28/4/1962	46163
18/10/1962	Eastleigh	L/Int	17/11/1962	55412

Withdrawn 14 July 1965.

C19 / 33019

Built at Ashford and outshopped in May 1942.

Sheds

First shed	Eastleigh
March 1944	Basingstoke
?	Eastleigh
May 1953	Ramsgate
July 1953	Guildford

Tender No.

As built	3159
20/2/1945	3170
1/6/1962	3174 *

Boiler Number

As built	1118
10/5/1951	1145
19/5/1955	1137
10/6/1958	1175

Repairs and Works visits	Works / Depot	Type of Repair	Returned to service	Mileage since last general repair
3/6/1943	Eastleigh	D	5/6/1943	22532
21/7/1943	Eastleigh	D	21/7/1943	
26/7/1943	Eastleigh	D	29/7/1943	
Eastleigh Shed		C	2/3/1944	42085
16/6/1944	Eastleigh	C	26/6/1944	46085
20/2/1945	Eastleigh	D	23/3/1945	61400
5/6/1945	Ashford	C	5/6/1945	57612
5/9/1945	Nine Elms		3/5/1945	
15/2/1946	Nine Elms	C	21/3/1946	83693
1/4/1948	Ashford	A	22/5/1948	117669
27/8/1948	Eastleigh	D	27/4/1948	1413
6/1/1949	Ashford	C	15/1/1949	3392
10/5/1951	Eastleigh	Gen	15/6/1951	53177
15/6/1953	Ashford	H/Int	4/7/1953	
19/5/1955	Ashford	Gen	19/8/1955	95336
8/9/1955	Ashford		24/9/1955	487
21/5/1957	Guildford		12/6/1957	45160
17/8/1957	Guildford		30/8/1957	50000
10/6/1958	Ashford	L/Int	28/6/1958	71415
7/10/1960	Ashford	Gen	29/10/1960	125709
25/7/1962	Eastleigh	L/Cas	18/8/1963	40821

* The tender change referred took place at Guildford Shed.

Withdrawn and reported as condemned on 7 December 1963. Scrapped on 1 February 1964.

33019 paused between shunting duties on the former Tongham branch and shortly before complete closure. This engine was reported as having modified driving axles fitted at Ashford on 25 May 1948 "on the advice of the CME." An unspecified test involving the leading and trailing axleboxes also took place at the same time.

David Lawrence / Hugh Davies

33020 in the last few months of its life, cautiously picking its way past a permanent way crew at Wimbledon on 21 September 1965.
R.K. Blencowe

C20 / 33020

Built at Ashford and outshopped on 6 May 1942.

Sheds

First shed	Eastleigh
March 1943	Guildford
March 1943	Basingstoke
July 1947	Eastleigh
June 1964	Feltham
November 1964	Guildford
June 1965	Nine Elms

Tender No.

As built	3160
19/5/1945	3150

Boiler Number

As built	1120
23/3/1950	1146
11/3/1954	1136
5/4/1960	1126

This engine was reported as being part AWS fitted only. It also had the more usual modifications of water treatment, a spark arrester (presumably WR type but not stated), and also pipes lagged.

Withdrawn January 1966.

Repairs and Works visits	Works / Depot	Type of Repair	Returned to service	Mileage since last general repair
28/7/1942	Eastleigh	D	31/7/1962	
29/8/1942	Ashford	D	29/8/1942	
19/11/1942	Eastleigh	C	24/11/1942	
14/1/1943	Eastleigh	D	18/1/1943	
24/8/1943	Eastleigh	D	22/8/1943	
17/10/1944	Eastleigh		25/11/1944	
5/3/1945	Ashford	D	17/3/1945	63305
19/5/1945	Nine Elms		19/5/1945	
27/7/1945	Guildford		27/9/1945	73361
22/2/1946	Nine Elms	C	22/2/1946	
25/4/1946	Nine Elms	C	14/4/1946	
20/8/1946	Nine Elms	C	28/4/1946	
28/12/1946	Ashford	A	1/2/1947	93252
23/3/1950	Ashford	A	21/4/1950	66000
22/5/1952	Ashford	Defect	12/6/1952	
17/6/1952	Ashford		25/6/1952	50207?
7/11/1952	Eastleigh	L/Cas	14/11/1952	57005
11/3/1954	Ashford	Gen	27/3/1954	88850
13/4/56	Ashford	L/Int	4/5/1956	44187
4/2/1957	Ashford	L/Cas	9/2/1957	61269
28/11/1957	Ashford	L/Cas	21/12/1957	78091
20/8/1958	Ashford	H/Int	6/9/1958	91395
10/6/1959	Eastleigh	N/C	20/6/1959	106944
7/8/1959	Eastleigh	L/Cas	21/8/1959	108168
5/4/60	Ashford	Gen	21/5/1960	120292
11/4/61	Eastleigh	L/Cas	22/4/1961	18888
9/2/62	Eastleigh Shed	N/C	24/2/1962	27525
8/3/63	Eastleigh /Shed	H/Int	13/4/1963	41098

C21 / 33021

Built at Ashford and outshopped on 22 May 1942 but did not enter service until the following month.

Sheds

First shed	Feltham
?	Guildford
March 1944	Basingstoke
September 1947	Eastleigh

Tender No.

As built	3160
19/5/1945	3150

Boiler Number

As built	1121
28/8/1950	1126
10/3/1955	1127
26/1/1960	1152

Withdrawn 24 August 1963.
Scrapped 26 October 1963.

Repairs and Works visits	Works / Depot	Type of Repair	Returned to service	Mileage since last general repair
29/8/1942	Ashford	D	29/8/1942	
30/4/1943	Eastleigh	D	3/5/1943	21728
6/9/1943	Eastleigh	D	15/9/1943	28557
28/4/1944	Ashford	D	26/5/1944	44515
12/5/1945	Ashford	B	31/5/1945	67080
30/10/1945	Nine Elms	C	1/11/1945	
30/9/1947	Ashford	A	31/10/1947	104480
17/2/1948	Eastleigh	D	21/2/1948	6091
28/8/1950	Ashford	H/Cas	22/9/1950	62559
24/9/1952	Ashford	H/Int	10/10/1952	108773
21/10/1952	Ashford	Defect	22/10/1952	
27/11/1952	Ashford	L/Cas	5/12/1952	109625
18/2/1954	Ashford	L/Cas	6/3/1954	137693
10/3/1955	Ashford	Gen	7/4/1955	159845
29/61956	Eastleigh	L/Cas	7/7/1956	29212
28/3/1957	Ashford	H/Int	18/4/1957	
23/1/1959	Ashford	L/Cas	6/2/1959	86471
26/1/1960	Ashford	Gen	20/2/1960	104204
5/5/1960	Ashford	N/C	4/6/1960	1030
9/3/1962	Eastleigh	N/C	17/3/1962	32063
11/6/1962	Guildford or Eastleigh?	L/Cas	17/7/1962	

33021 on what is probably an empty stock working entering Brockenhurst from the west on 17 August 1959. This engine received the complete list of modifications, pipes lagged, AWS, spark arrester, modified cab doors, safety links, mechanical lubricator, protector glass, and side windows.
R.S. Carpenter

33022 seemingly fresh from overhaul - Ashford 1952 perhaps? This particular machine is not believed to have many if any, additions aside from the smokebox handrails fitted to all the class. It was also only the subject of a single test involving differing size valve and piston rings.

C22 / 33022

Built at Ashford and outshopped on 11 June 1942.

Sheds

First shed	Feltham
?	Guildford
March 1944	Basingstoke
September ?	Eastleigh
March 1953	Ramsgate

Tender No.

As built	3162
4/4/1946	3145
21/3/1952	3174
1/6/1962	3170*
24/4/1963	3173*

*Both tender changes took place at Guildford Loco.

Boiler Number

As built	1126
21/3/1952	1150
22/3/1956	1123
11/5/1961	1172

Repairs and Works visits	Works / Depot	Type of Repair	Returned to service	Mileage since last general repair
13/1/1943	Eastleigh	D	21/1/1943	9664
15/7/1943	Eastleigh	D	21/7/1943	23909
11/10/1943	Eastleigh	D	15/10/1943	30116
4/4/1946	Nine Elms	C	4/4/1946	
31/8/1946	Ashford	A	11/10/1946	86475
10/2/1947	Eastleigh	D	15/2/1947	4465
8/8/1947	Nine Elms	C	8/8/1947	
17/9/1947	Eastleigh	D	23/9/1947	15760
22/11/1947	Eastleigh		29/11/1947	18737
12/1/1950	Ashford	L/Int	10/2/1950	60288
21/3/1952	Ashford	Gen	10/4/1952	107499
30/4/1954	Ashford	H/Int	15/5/1954	51606
4/11/1954	Ashford	L/Cas	22/11/1954	64329
22/3/1956	Ashford	Gen	14/4/1956	89345
14/8/1956	Ashford	N/C	18/8/1956	
15/5/1957	Ashford	L/Cas	26/5/1957	25011
30/12/1957	Ashford	L/Cas	18/1/1958	39663
18/2/1959	Ashford	L/I	7/3/1959	68628
11/5/1961	Ashford	Gen	10/6/1961	119334

Withdrawn 5 January 1964.

ECS working into Bournemouth Central on 3 April 1959 and in charge of 33023. The angle of the photograph shows that the contours of the tender matched the Bulleid coaching stock well. Unlike with the Pacific type none of the Q1s had the sides of the tender cut down in later years.

Roger Carpenter

C23 / 33023

Built at Ashford and outshopped in June 1942.

Sheds

First shed	Feltham
?	Guildford
March 1944	Eastleigh

Tender No.

As built	3163

Boiler Number

As built	1125
24/11/1958	1130

Repairs and Works visits	Works / Depot	Type of Repair	Returned to service	Mileage since last general repair
21/5/1943	Eastleigh	B	25/5/1943	16195
at Feltham	Eastleigh			
22/6/1944	Eastleigh	D	22/6/1944	34295
		Weighing		
27/10/1950	Eastleigh	Weighing	27/10/1950	43797
9/1/1951	Eastleigh	L/Cas	12/1/1951	46051
1/5/191952	Eastleigh	L/Cas	10/5/1952	72934
24/11/1958	Ashford	Gen	13/12/1958	105170
23/7/1959	Ashford	N/C	8/8/1959	8880
16/11/1959	Ashford	L/Cas	28/11/1959	14680
17/3/1960	Ashford	L/Cas	31/3/1960	18719
23/1/1961	Guildford	L/Cas	8/2/1961	
10/11/1961	Eastleigh	H/Int	2/12/1961	50000

Withdrawn 14 June 1964.

The final stages of overhaul at Ashford on 2 August 1950 and not long before a return to traffic. The engine had been renumbered as shown on 17 March 1949 and was also the subject of three tests involving figure of 8 oil grooves in axleboxes, axle bearings with rolled finish and heat resisting firebars. These may all have commenced in 1945. New cylinders were also fitted in February / March 1948. From a regular servicing perspective one of the major drawbacks of the class was the very narrow space to stand on the above the buffer beam when cleaning the smokebox and it became practice to place a plank across the buffers to assist.   J.H. Aston

C24 / 33024

Built at Ashford and outshopped on 26 June 1942.

Sheds	
First shed	Feltham
March 1944	Guildford
December 1947	Eastleigh
October 1953	Tonbridge
January 1961	Feltham
September 1962	Three Bridges

Tender No.	
As built	3164
18/4/1944	3166 *

* not stated where this exchange took place.

Boiler Number	
As built	1128
24/12/1951	1116
14/6/1957	1122

Repairs and Works visits	Works / Depot	Type of Repair	Returned to service	Mileage since last general repair
7/11/1942	Eastleigh	D	18/11/1942	7489
16/7/1943	Eastleigh	D	27/7/1943	24957
1/11/1945	Eastleigh	A	1/12/1945	68475
25/9/1946	Nine Elms	C	25/9/1946	
24/2/1947	Ashford	D	10/4/1947	25207
15/9/1947	Nine Elms		15/9/1947	
9/2/1948	Eastleigh	B	3/4/1948	36272
17/3/1949	Eastleigh	L/Cas	5/3/1949	51974
10/7/1950	Ashford	L/Int	9/8/1950	79353
24/12/1951	Ashford	Gen	24/1/1952	104240
31/1/1952	Ashford	Defect	31/1/1952	
11/2/1952	Ashford	Defect	13/2/1952	
6/3/1952	Ashford	Defect	14/3/1952	
19/3/1954	Ashford	H/Int	3/4/1954	40682
7/9/1954	Ashford	N/C	18/9/1954	51621
23/12/1955	Ashford	H/Int	14/1/1956	77991
14/6/1957	Ashford	Gen	6/7/1957	108228
3/4/1958	Ashford	N/C	19/4/1958	18044
10/6/1959	Ashford	H/Int	27/6/1959	46823
30/11/1959	Ashford	N/C	19/12/1959	59751
20/9/1961	Eastleigh	L/Cas	14/12/1961	107398

Withdrawn 25 August 1963.
Sold 7 March 1964.

C25 / 33025

Built at Ashford and outshopped on 3 July 1942.

Sheds

First shed	Feltham
March 1944	Guildford
December 1947	Eastleigh
June 1954	Nine Elms
July 1954	Guildford

Tender No.

As built	3165
24/11/1945	3176 *
19/9/1955	3144
16/9/1959	3151

*tender exchange at Ashford

Boiler Number

As built	1129
1/2/1951	1133
19/9/1955	1115
25/10/1960	1133

Repairs and Works visits	Works / Depot	Type of Repair	Returned to service	Mileage since last general repair
2/1/1943	Eastleigh	D	12/1/1943	7982
21/5/1943	Eastleigh	D	26/5/1943	17129
22/9/1943	Eastleigh	D	28/9/1943	25218
18/5/1944	Eastleigh	B	18/8/1944	41823
31/8/1944	Eastleigh	C	27/9/1944	41858
14/10/1944	Eastleigh	C	11/11/1944	42026
19/10/1945	Eastleigh	C	14/11/1945	68529
6/7/1946	Nine Elms	C	8/7/1946	
24/7/1947	Ashford	A	30/8/1947	93437
18/5/1948	Eastleigh	D	20/5/1948	7785
1/2/1951	Ashford	Gen	2/3/1951	
9/3/1941	Ashford	Defect	?/3/1951	63028
	Ashford	Defect	24/3/1951	
27/3/1951	Ashford	Defect	4/4/1951	
4/5/1951	Ashford	?	10/5/1951	
30/4/1953	Ashford	H/Int	21/5/1953	
3/6/1953		Defect		
19/9/1955	Ashford	Gen	8/10/1955	103414
20/9/1957	Guildford		12/10/1957	49648
5/9/1958	Ashford	L/Int	27/9/1958	71863
16/9/1959	Ashford	L/Cas	10/1/0/1959	1001709
25/10/1962	Ashford	Gen	26/11/1960	119448
7/12/1962	Eastleigh	N/C	19/12/1962	45135

Withdrawn 7 July 1963.
Scrapped 22 February 1964.

A grimy 33025 at Eastleigh on 25 February 1950. Records are contradictory for this engine as far as renumbering is concerned as one source states 33025 together with 33019 were the first of the class to receive BR numbers at Ashford in April 1948, yet the engine record card for 33025 states this did not take place until 1 February 1951. By the time the view had been taken the engine had been fitted with 'Vesuvius' heat resisting fire bars, added at Eastleigh Shed in April 1948. Notice the sliding shutters attached to the tender and which most of the class retained until withdrawal. Tony Sedgwick

C26 in a temporarily embarrassing situation, the location not recorded. Most minor incidents such as this could be readily resolved with jacks and packing rather than recourse to a crane. Notice the amount of small coal that has found its way to the base of the tender and no doubt due to the precarious angle.

C26 / 33026

Built at Ashford and outshopped on 29 July 1942.

Sheds

First shed	Feltham
December 1947	Tonbridge
November 1950	Gillingham
August 1951	Tonbridge
July 1953	Feltham
September 1962	Three Bridges
December 1963	Feltham
November 1964	Guildford
June 1965	Nine Elms

Tender No.

As built	3166
7/12/1944	3156
17/8/1945	3175
2/10/1952	3160

Boiler Number

As built	1131
27/4/1950	1175
24/2/1956	1114

Repairs and Works visits	Works / Depot	Type of Repair	Returned to service	Mileage since last general repair
7/12/1944	Ashford	D	16/12/1944	
17/8/1945	Ashford	D	25/8/1945	55302
7/2/1946	Feltham	C	12/3/1946	
11/2/1947	Ashford	A	22/3/1947	80216
28/10/1947	Ashford	D	5/12/1947	11714
3/3/1949	Ashford	H/Int	2/4/1949	31380
27/4/1950	Ashford	Gen	26/5/1950	56301
4/12/1951	Ashford	L/Cas	9/12/1951	
2/10/1952	Ashford	H/Int	17/10/1952	44651
5/11/1954	Brighton	H/Cas	7/12/1954	
24/2/1956	Ashford	Gen	17/3/1956	104489
1/4/1958	Ashford	L/Int	26/4/1958	49424
27/7/1960	Ashford	Gen	23/8/1960	101853
21/5/1963	Eastleigh	H/Int	15/6/1963	47765

Renumbered as BR 33026 in April 1949.
Withdrawn September 1965.

33027 shunting at North Camp (Aldershot) on 23 April 1955 and what is clearly a local pick-up goods working. Only one test is known of for this engine, variations to the size of the rings, indeed could it be that all the class were so tested and in fact it became a modification?

Norman Simmons / Hugh Davies

C27 / 33027

Built at Ashford and outshopped on 29 July 1942.

Sheds

First shed	Feltham
December 1947	Tonbridge
April 1951	Gillingham
August 1951	Tonbridge
July 1953	Feltham
November 1964	?
June 1965	Nine Elms
October 1965	Guildford

Tender No.

As built	3167
17/10/1942	3146
14/4/1944	1172

Boiler Number

As built	1133
26/9/1950	1140
23/4/1954	1132
29/2/1960	1138

Repairs and Works visits	Works / Depot	Type of Repair	Returned to service	Mileage since last general repair
3/9/1942	Eastleigh	D	5/9/1942	
17/10/1942	Ashford	D	3/11/1942	5159
14/4/1944	Ashford	D	6/5/1944	41206
9/8/1945	Ashford	C	31/8/1945	69412
16/7/1946	Ashford	A	12/9/1946	87130
18/3/1947	Nine Elms	C	18/3/1947	
1/6/1948	Ashford	B	1/7/1948	32208
26/9/1950	Ashford	Gen	20/10/1950	12094
3/7/1952	Ashford	H/Int	25/7/1952	32908
23/4/1954	Ashford	Gen	15/5/1954	72530
2/3/1956	Ashford	H/Int	22/3/1956	41791
20/10/1956	Redhill		25/11/1956	
27/7/1957	Redhill		22/8/1957	69826
8/5/1958	Ashford	H/Int	24/5/1958	88153
5/10/1959	Ashford	Cas	24/10/1959	117809
29/2/1960	Ashford	Gen	26/3/1960	122178
13/10/1962	Eastleigh	L/Int		44346

Withdrawn 9 January 1966.

33028 at what is believed to be part of the original shed at Tonbridge. Several members of the class had short term moves to Tonbridge and other south eastern depots around 1953 in order to work spoil and ballast trains in connection with necessary repairs caused by dramatic coastal flooding of that year. Not all these moves were necessarily recorded. This particular engine is known to have received water treatment, lagged pipes, AWS and as can also be seen cab protectors. The latter apparently fitted very early on. This was also the first of the class to be withdrawn.

C28 / 33028

Built at Ashford and outshopped on 29 August 1942.

Sheds

First shed	Feltham
December 1947	Tonbridge
November 1950	Gillingham
August 1951	Tonbridge
January 1961	Feltham
September 1962	Three Bridges

Tender No.

As built	3168
13/1/1943	3161
11/9/1952	3145
9/2/1963	3177 *

* Exchange took place at Eastleigh Shed.

Boiler Number

As built	1135
6/2/1951	1142
2/9/1954	1146
14/11/1857	1149

Withdrawn 9 February 1963.
Scrapped 9 March 1963.

Repairs and Works visits	Works / Depot	Type of Repair	Returned to service	Mileage since last general repair
13/1/1943	Eastleigh	D	16/1/1943	5603
29/4/1943	Eastleigh	D	1/5/1943	11702
5/7/1943	Eastleigh	D	7/7/1943	13890
28/7/1943	Feltham			
1/5/1945	Ashford	C	2/6/1945	56538
29/10/1945	Nine Elms	C	29/10/1955	
8/12/1945	Ashford	C	11/1/1946	69921
23/12/1946	Ashford	A	1/2/1947	82212
18/10/1948	Ashford	C	13/11/1948	23519
New Cross Gate			7/5/1949	30558
6/2/1951	Ashford	Gen	2/3/1951	76626
11/9/1952	Ashford	H/Int	2/6/1952	28895
24/11/1953	Ashford	L/Cas	10/12/1953	50983
2/9/1954	Ashford	H/Cas	25/9/1954	64302
7/10/1955	Ashford	H/Int	17/10/1955	89142
4/12/1956	Brighton	L/Cas	22/12/1956	113434
14/11/1957	Ashford	Gen	14/12/1957	138224
22/4/1959	Ashford	L/Int	16/5/1959	40912
27/10/1960	Ashford	L/Cas	19/11/1960	38797
24/10/1961	Eastleigh	H/Int	11/11/1961	63562

C29 / 33029

Built at Ashford and outshopped on
16 September 1962.

Sheds	
First shed	Feltham
December 1947	Tonbridge
May 1962	Feltham
September 1962	Three Bridges

Tender No.	
As built	3169
2/9/1944	3179
22/5/1945	3159

Boiler Number	
As built	1137
27/6/1951	1129

*   a fractured left hand cylinder was
     replaced at this time.

Withdrawn 5 January 1964.

Repairs and Works visits	Works / Depot	Type of Repair	Returned to service	Mileage since last general repair
6/5/1943	Eastleigh	D	10/5/1943	14406
13/7/1944	Feltham		25/7/1944	
2/9/44	Eastleigh	C	23/9/1944	43902
26/1/1945	Nine Elms		26/1/1945	
22/5/1945	Nine Elms		22/5/1945	
19/11/1945	Nine Elms	C	9/11/1945	
17/12/1945	Nine Elms	C	18/12/1945	
12/2/1946	Nine Elms	C	13/2/1946	
27/3/1946	Ashford	B	4/5/1946	83381
10/1/1947	Nine Elms *	C	13/1/1947	
12/7/1947	Ashford	A	28/8/1947	107053
14/11/1948	Tonbridge	C	22/12/1948	
16/3/1950	Ashford	H/Cas	31/3/1950	49206
27/6/1951	Ashford	Gen	20/7/1957	67054
2/8/1951	Ashford	Defect	8/8/1951	
26/6/1952	Ashford	L/Cas	11/7/1952	25435
4/3/1953	Ashford	H/Int	20/3/1953	38589
27/11/1953	Ashford	L/Cas	19/12/1953	
2/12/1954	Ashford	L/Cas	16/12/1954	
7/6/1955	Ashford	Gen	29/6/1955	
20/10/1955	Ashford	L/Cas	21/10/1955	
19/6/1957	Ashford	H/Int	6/7/1957	
16/4/1958	Ashford	N/Cas	26/4/1958	
29/9/1959	Ashford	Gen	7/11/1959	
16/11/1959	Ashford	N/Cas	28/11/1959	
22/6/1961	Ashford	H/Int	22/7/1961	

C29 raising steam ready for work. Aside from the usual changes and modifications as might be expected, lagged pipes, water treatment, a briquette container, safety link gear, AWS and spark arrestor, all added at various unspecified times, there is an interesting reference in the records to 'handrails removed'. No further information is available to elaborate on this entry.

C30 at Redhill on 22 May 1948 and for the present retaining the tender water fillers located within the cab. One of these cab be seen in the highlighted enlargement. It would appear all of the tenders were subsequently modified with a conventional water filler at the rear. Those in the cab being simply blanked off. The date of this change is not recorded for any of the tenders. Renumbered as BR 33030 at Ashford on 12 August 1948, the same date is recorded as the start of axlebox trails (unspecified), and modified anti-carbonisers. J.H. Aston

C30 / 33030

Built at Ashford and outshopped on 23 September 1942.

Sheds	
First shed	Feltham
December 1947	Tonbridge
May 1962	Nine Elms
December 1963	Three Bridges

Tender No.	
As built	3151
2/5/1944	3159
29/8/1952	3153

Boiler Number	
As built	1139
29/8/1952	1148
27/10/1957	1141

Withdrawn 14 June 1962.

Repairs and Works visits	Works / Depot	Type of Repair	Returned to service	Mileage since last general repair
6/10/1943	Eastleigh	D	13/10/1943	24558
2/5/1944	Eastleigh	C	12/5/1944	38959
13/4/1945	Feltham	C	16/4/1945	
22/5/1945	Nine Elms	C	23/5/1945	
6/7/1945	Ashford	C	18/8/1945	63668
12/12/1945	Nine Elms	C	13/12/1945	
31/1/1946	Nine Elms	C	1/2/1946	
9/4/1946	Ashford	C	28/5/1946	77237
5/1/1947	Guildford	C	17/2/1947	
29/9/1947	Nine Elms		30/9/1947	
29/10/1947	Nine Elms		3/11/1947	
29/6/1948	Ashford	A	12/8/1948	110345
12/10/1950	Ashford	H/Int	10/11/1950	45510
29/8/1952	Ashford	Gen	2/1/1953	
9/1/1953	Ashford	Defect	14/1/1953	
3/12/1954	Ashford	L/Cas	17/12/1954	38366
23/9/1955	Ashford	H/Int	29/10/1955	56936
27/10/1957	Ashford	Gen	23/11/1957	92340
6/2/1958	Ashford	Return	15/2/1958	2476
30/6/1959	Ashford	L/Cas	18/7/1959	42494
25/9/1959	Ashford	L/Cas	17/10/1959	48672
1/6/1961	Ashford	L/Int	1/7/1961	79085
6/3/1963	Eastleigh	L/Cas	9/3/1963	108709

33031 at Ashford. But displaying a Tonbridge shed code. The usual modifications were carried by this engine including safety links, AWS, protector glasses to the cab, spark arrestor, modified gangway doors, and lagged pipes.

R. Blencowe

C31 / 33031

Built at Ashford and outshopped on 12 October 1942.

Sheds	
First shed	Feltham
April 1948	Tonbridge
May 1962	Nine Elms
November 1962	Three Bridges

Tender No.	
As built	3170
18/8/1943	3149
21/4/1944	3174
13/3/1952	3145
16/7/1952	1959

Boiler Number	
As built	1141
26/2/1953	1149
7/2/1957	1118

Repairs and Works visits	Works / Depot	Type of Repair	Returned to service	Mileage since last general repair
18/8/1943	Eastleigh	D	20/8/1943	17603
28/9/1943	Eastleigh	D	29/9/1943	20983
3/2/1944	Eastleigh	C	4/3/1944	27013
21/4/1944	Eastleigh	C	2/5/1944	31743
15/8/1944	Eastleigh	C	31/8/1944	38625
27/8/1945	Nine Elms	C	31/8/1945	60572
29/1/1946	Feltham	C	25/2/1946	
17/4/1947	Ashford	A	17/5/1947	85404
10/6/1949	Ashford	H/Cas	9/7/1949	39534
18/10/1950	Ashford	H/Int	17/11/1950	64090
13/3/1952	Ashford	H/Int	25/4/1952	87273
16/7/1952	Ashford	L/Cas	1/8/1952	89782
26/2/1953	Ashford	Gen	13/3/1953	100456
16/7/1954	Ashford	L/Cas	4/8/1954	30736
7/2/1957	Ashford	Gen	2/3/1957	79522
29/5/1958	Ashford	L/Cas	14/6/1958	29313
21/1/1959	Ashford	H/Int	14/2/1959	49264
1/6/1960	Ashford	H/Int	2/7/1960	82605
7/12/1961	Eastleigh	L/Cas	30/12/1961	124691

Withdrawn 5 October 1963.

33032 on loco duty 315. This turn commenced at Tonbridge at 3.45 am. Running light engine from the shed to Tonbridge West Yard ready for the 4.08 am freight to Hastings. After shunting, another freight was worked to Ore returning again to Hastings for 11.40 am. Then run light to St. Leonards loco before working another freight to Battle. The engine finally returned to Tonbridge shed at 7.16 pm. Two crews were involved in the turn.

C32 / 33032

Built at Ashford and outshopped on 28 October 1942.

Sheds

First shed	Feltham
April 1948	Tonbridge
May 1962	Guildford

Tender No.

As built	3172
24/5/1945	3149
4/6/1952	3171

Boiler Number

As built	1143
4/6/1952	1128
23/8/1955	1120
14/4/1959	1125

Repairs and Works visits	Works / Depot	Type of Repair	Returned to service	Mileage since last general repair
31/5/1943	Eastleigh	D	7/6/1943	10482
24/5/1945	Ashford	C	15/6/1945	59615
23/7/1945	Ashford	D	1/9/1945	59714
15/9/1945	Ashford	D	1/11/1945	59862
16/4/1946	Ashford	D	18/4/1946	67298
24/5/1946	Ashford	A	27/6/1946	83858
15/4/1948	Bricklayers Arms	D	16/4/1948	14340
1/12/1948	Ashford		8/1/1949	28251
13/7/1949	Ashford	L/Int	13/8/1949	39271
15/12/1950	Ashford	H/Int	18/1/1951	69637
4/6/1952	Ashford	Gen	20/6/1952	100948
11/6/1953	Ashford	H/Int	2/7/1953	
13/12/1954	Ashford	H/C	1/1/1955	58434
23/8/1955	Ashford	Gen	12/9/1955	67617
18/1/1957	Ashford	H/Int	8/2/1957	17741
25/3/1958	Brighton	L/Int	25/4/1958	
14/4/1959	Ashford	Gen	8/5/1959	82372
27/6/1960	Ashford	L/Cas	30/7/1960	30003
29/9/1961	Eastleigh	H/Int	21/10/1961	8370
31/5/1962	Eastleigh	N/C	9/6/1962	72564

Withdrawn 5 January 1964.
Scrapped 14 March 1964.

C33 / 33033

Built at Ashford and outshopped on
11 November 1942.

Sheds

First shed	Feltham
April 1948	Tonbridge
May 1962	Guildford

Tender No.

As built	3173
27/5/52	3155

Boiler Number

As built	1145
2/10/50	1134
31/1/1955	1138
26/1/1960	1152
23/9/1959	1116

Withdrawn 14 June 1964.

Repairs and Works visits	Works / Depot	Type of Repair	Returned to service	Mileage since last general repair
2/6/1943	Eastleigh	D	7/6/1943	6414
27/7/1943	Feltham			
2/8/1944	Eastleigh	C	4/8/1944	38653
24/5/1945	Ashford	C	14/6/1945	62393
1/3/1946	Nine Elms	C	4/3/1946	
2/7/1946	Eastleigh	A	17/8/1946	85830
30/9/1947	Nine Elms		2/10/1947	
2/6/1948	Ashford	C	3/7/1948	32755
14/2/1949	Ashford	L/Cas	24/3/1949	44938
29/9/1949	Ashford	N/C	29/9/1949	57965
2/10/1950	Ashford	H/Cas	27/10/1950	79512
27/5/1952	Ashford	H/Int	18/6/1952	114164
26/8/1953	Ashford	L/Cas	12/9/1953	138490
15/6/1954	Brighton	L/Cas	2/7/1954	
31/1/1955	Ashford	Gen	21/2/1955	162601
7/9/1956	Ashford	N/C	26/9/1956	35653
23/8/1957	Ashford	L/Int	14/9/1957	56302
18/3/1958	Ashford	N/C	24/3/1958	71117
23/9/1959	Ashford	Gen	17/10/1959	112139
5/11/1959		N/C	21/11/1959	
1/11/1961	Eastleigh	H/Int	2/12/1961	47534

Tonbridge yard in 1961 and 33033 keeps company amidst a variety of former South Eastern, Southern and BR types. Only one test is known of for this engine and involving piston rings in 1946. There is also no record of AWS or other modifications being fitted.

R. Blencowe

A very grimy 33034 runs light through Tonbridge on 4 June 1958. According to the records there were no works or other major repairs carried out to this engine in 1958 although normal maintenance would of course have taken place. The front coupling is also seen correctly hooked out of use, not all crews bothering to do this.

Roger Carpenter

C34 / 33034

Built at Ashford and outshopped on 22 November 1942.

Sheds

First shed	Feltham
April 1948	Tonbridge
May 1961	Guildford

Tender No.

As built	3174
25/4/1944	3149
24/4/1945	3144
14/9/1955	3176

Boiler Number

As built	1147
10/3/1952	1137
13/6/1952	1117
9/5/1957	1174

Repairs and Works visits	Works / Depot	Type of Repair	Returned to service	Mileage since last general repair
28/11/1942	Ashford	DEA?	29/11/1942	
21/4/1943	Eastleigh	D	30/4/1943	7817
25/4/1944	Eastleigh	C	2/5/1944	28641
24/4/1945	Ashford	D	5/5/1945	59974
20/9/1945	Stewarts Lane	C	8/11/1945	61453
5/9/1947	Ashford	A	10/10/1947	94368
21/3/1949	Ashford	L/Int	22/4/1949	41799
26/12/1949	Tonbridge		24/1/1950	
10/7/1950	Ashford	L/Cas	4/8/1950	56867
10/1/1951	Ashford		18/1/1951	66665
10/3/1952	Ashford	Gen	28/3/1952	86486
13/6/1952	Ashford	Retn?	4/7/1952	1626
3/7/1953	Ashford	L/Cas	1/8/1953	
7/10/1954	Ashford	H/C	22/10/1954	37162
14/9/1955	Ashford	H/Int	5/10/1955	54669
15/2/1957	Ashford	H/C	22/2/1957	89692
9/5/1957	Ashford	Gen	1/6/1957	85134
10/10/1957	Ashford	N/C	17/10/1957	2409
2/3/1959	Ashford	L/Cas	14/3/1959	40919
25/6/1959	Ashford	L/Cas	11/7/1959	48248
11/4/1961	Ashford	H/Int	6/5/1961	93674
25/1/1962	Ashford	L/Cas	17/2/1962	109275

Withdrawn 5 January 1964.

33035 passing Wadhurst in the 1950's. As has been reported elsewhere from 8 September 1945 until May 1946 a member of the class was temporarily attached to a West Country tender and a duplicate set of remote controls fitted. According to Bradley this involved C36 although the record card for C35 refers to this fitment with no mention on the corresponding card for C36. The equipment was later removed and no photographs appear to have survived of the fittings.

Roger Carpenter

C35 / 33035

Built at Ashford and outshopped on 30 November 1942.

Sheds

First shed	Feltham
April 1948	Tonbridge
May 1961	Guildford

Tender No.

As built	3171
21/4/1952	3149

Boiler Number

As built	1149
21/4/1952	1118
23/2/1956	1172
21/11/1960	1119

Repairs and Works visits	Works / Depot	Type of Repair	Returned to service	Mileage since last general repair
27/5/1943	Eastleigh	D	1/6/1943	8754
19/3/1945	Feltham	C	4/4/1945	
26/4/1945	Ashford	D	5/5/1945	
21/5/1946	Ashford	B	3/7/1946	71808
26/9/1946	Nine Elms	C	26/9/1946	
22/3/1948	Ashford	A	30/4/1948	102600
8/7/1949	Ashford	N/C	8/7/1949	22514
19/9/1950	Ashford	H/Int	13/10/1950	48376
12/12/1951	Ashford	N/C	21/12/1951	
21/4/1952	Ashford	Gen	27/6/1952	84652
2/7/1953	Ashford	L/Cas	22/7/1953	26384
8/11/1954	Ashford	L/Int	25/1/1954	55701
23/2/1956	Ashford	Gen	17/3/1956	82906
1/8/1957	Ashford	L/Cas	10/8/1957	26242
2/1/1958	Ashford	L/Int	18/1/1958	35931
3/12/1958	Ashford	L/Cas	13/12/1958	57116
24/4/1959	Ashford	L/Cas	30/5/1959	65640
31/8/1959	Ashford	N/C	16/9/1959	66180
21/11/1960	Ashford	Gen	17/12/1960	93248
15/5/1962	Eastleigh	L/Cas	9/6/1962	30475

Withdrawn 14 June 1964.

Together with Tonbridge, Feltham and Eastleigh, Guildford was one of the best locations to witness the class at work and at rest, 33036 seen at the Surrey junction the steam escaping from the reverser. N. Hamshere

C36 / 33036

Built at Ashford and outshopped on 16 December 1942.

Subject to figure 8 axlebox test with mechanical lubricators fitted to coupled axleboxes on 28/10/1948.

Renumbered at Ashford Works on 28/10/1948.

Sheds	
First shed	Feltham
April 1948	Stewarts Lane
January 1950	Tonbridge
July 1951	Stewarts Lane
September 1952	Tonbridge
May 1961	Guildford

Tender No.	
As built	3175
25/8/1945	3256
4/4/1946	3155
23/7/1951	3173
19/8/1961	3144 *

Boiler Number	
As built	1151
10/12/1952	1139
4/3/1958	1143

Repairs and Works visits	Works / Depot	Type of Repair	Returned to service	Mileage since last general repair
30/8/1943	Eastleigh	D	4/9/1943	15572
2/5/1944	Eastleigh	C	12/5/1944	30379
7/7/1944	Eastleigh	C	15/7/1944	34222
29/3/1945	Ashford	D	13/4/1945	51049
Ashford	New	25/8/1945		
9/8/1945	Ashford	D	8/9/1945	60067
4/4/1946	Ashford	C	23/5/1946	70237
19/10/1946	Ashford	B	22/11/1946	77167
12/7/1947	Ashford	C	9/8/1947	87560
30/3/1948	Feltham		19/4/1948	96856
16/9/1948	Ashford	A	28/10/1948	102731
25/4/1949	Ashford	N/C	14/5/1949	9265
2/6/1950	Tonbridge		5/7/1950	
13/11/1950	Ashford	H/Cas	12/1/1951	41207
25/7/1951	Ashford	L/Cas	10/8/1951	50718
10/12/1952	Ashford	Gen	9/1/1953	73765
3/3/1954	Ashford	L/Cas	6/3/1954	19478
23/7/1954	Ashford	Return	6/8/1954	28124
13/10/1954	Redhill?	L/Int	16/11/1954	
24/2/1955	Ashford	L/Cas	12/3/1955	35920
12/11/1956	Ashford	H/Int	30/11/1956	67934
4/3/1958	Ashford	Gen	22/3/1958	96305
8/6/1959	Ashford	L/Cas	27/6/1959	30667
18/3/1960	Ashford	H/Int	16/4/1960	50100
28/3/1961	Ashford	L/Cas	22/4/1961	75010
	Guildford		19/8/1961	
5/2/1963	Eastleigh	L/Int	2/3/1963	110414

Withdrawn 28 June 1964.

C37 photographed in 1947. The note on the back refers to the location being Stratford although it looks far more like Eastleigh Works! Renumbered by BR in August 1948 this engine also received the full amount of modifications, pipes lagged AWS, spark arrestor, protector glass to the side windows, blowdown gear and silencer and a briquette tube feeder. There is also a comment stating that the tender handrails had been renewed, but this would of course depend to which tender it was attached at the time and no dates are given.

C37 / 33037

Built at Brighton and outshopped on 27 November 1942.

Sheds

First shed	Feltham
April 1948	Stewarts Lane
January 1950	Tonbridge
July 1951	Stewarts Lane
September 1952	Hither Green
April 1954	Brighton
October 1954	Hither Green
May 1959	Tonbridge
May 1961	Eastleigh

Tender No.

As built	3177
9/2/1963	3145 *

* tender exchanged at Eastleigh Shed.

Boiler Number

As built	1148
26/8/1952	1144
23/8/1956	1175
9/6/1960	1136

Withdrawn 24 August 1963.
Scrapped 26 october 1963.

Repairs and Works visits	Works / Depot	Type of Repair	Returned to service	Mileage since last general repair
24/5/1944	Ashford	D	17/7/1944	39439
24/1/1945	Nine Elms	C	25/1/1945	
7/6/1945	Feltham	C	24/6/1945	
21/5/1946	Ashford	B	3/7/1946	75827
20/8/1946	Ashford	D	21/9/1946	77417
19/11/1947	Nine Elms		21/11/1947	
10/1/1948	Nine Elms	D	17/1/1948	
20/5/1948	Ashford	A	24/7/1948	107603
15/3/1949	Stewarts Lane	N/C	7/4/1949	
25/10/1950	Ashford	N/C	25/10/1950	
1/1/1951	Ashford	L/Int	2/2/1951	46413
26/8/1952	Ashford	Gen	10/10/1952	77917
6/5/1954	Ashford	H/Int	22/5/1954	44502
2/6/1954	Ashford	Defect	3/6/1954	44563
2/11/1955	Ashford	L/Cas	5/11/1955	70880
23/8/1956	Ashford	Gen	14/9/1956	86182
2/6/1968	Ashford	H/Int	21/6/1958	42385
9/6/1960	Ashford	Gen	16/7/1960	74722
18/6/1962	Eastleigh	L/Cas	7/7/1962	41045

33038 shunting at what may well be in the Tunbridge Wells area - the wagon brake though is clearly on! This was one of only a few engines to be tested with figure of 8 oil grooves in 1946 and at the same time drainage of the axlebox keeps. Additionally the gudgeon pin was fitted with circlips, and a stiffening plate added behind the buffer beam in the same year. This latter feature is believed to have been unique to this engine. The other usual changes also occurred, spark arrestor, water treatment, blow-down gear and silencer, briquette tube feeder, AWS, protector glass and pipes lagged.

C38 / 33038

Built at Brighton Ashford and outshopped on 8 December 1942.

Reported as having new cylinders on 27 April 1946 although there is no works visit mentioned at that time.

Sheds

First shed	Feltham
April 1948	Stewarts Lane
January 1950	Tonbridge
July 1951	Stewarts Lane
September 1952	Eastleigh
June 1954	Norwood Junction
October 1954	Stewarts Lane
January 1955	Eastleigh
?	Feltham

Tender No.

As built	3176
21/6/1943	3167
15/2/1945	3151
24/10/1952	3180

Boiler Number

As built	1150
27/7/1951	1122
24/8/1956	1135

Repairs and Works visits	Works / Depot	Type of Repair	Returned to service	Mileage since last general repair
21/6/1943	Eastleigh	D	28/6/1943	
6/9/1943	Eastleigh	D	11/9/1943	16049
15/2/1945	Ashford	C	13/3/1945	56435
28/12/1945	Eastleigh	A	27/4/1946	67988
30/11/1948	Ashford	B	1/1/1949	51428
15/11/1949	Ashford	L/Cas	25/11/1949	70432
5/10/1949	Ashford	N/C	10/10/1949	
16/7/1950	Tonbridge		14/9/1950	
27/7/1951	Ashford	Gen	7/9/1951	
5/10/1951	Ashford	Defect	8/10/1951	
24/10/1952	Ashford	H/I	5/12/1952	26211
28/6/1954	Ashford	H/I	17/7/1954	59198
24/8/1956	Ashford	Gen	15/9/1956	107872
21/8/1958	Ashford	H/Int	6/9/1958	44235
3/3/1960	Ashford	H/I	26/3/1960	80254
3/11/1960	Ashford	N/C	12/11/1960	56026
24/4/1961	Ashford	L/Cas	12/5/1961	95248
13/9/1961	Eastleigh	L/Cas	7/10/1961	99540
10/10/1962	Eastleigh	L/Cas	3/11/1962	111862

Withdrawn 11 January 1964. Scrapped 1 February 1964.

C39 / 33039

Built at Brighton and outshopped on 15 December 1942 .

Sheds

First shed	Feltham
April 1948	Stewarts Lane
July 1950	?
July 1957	Hither Green
May 1959	Tonbridge
May 1961	Eastleigh

Tender No.

As built	3178

Boiler Number

As built	1152
30/1/1953	1143
8/7/1957	1144

Withdrawn 14 June 1964.

Repairs and Works visits	Works / Depot	Type of Repair	Returned to service	Mileage since last general repair
15/5/1943	Eastleigh	D	20/5/1943	
23/7/1943	Eastleigh	D	27/7/1943	13284
26/3/1945	Ashford	D	30/3/1945	55639
26/6/1945	Ashford	C	11/8/1945	61960
8/2/1946	Nine Elms	C	8/2/1946	
3/12/1946	Ashford	A	11/1/1947	86517
27/7/1947	Nine Elms	C	2/8/1947	
16/11/1948	Ashford	B	18/12/1948	32681
27/4/1950	Ashford	L/Cas	19/5/1950	49282
15/3/1951	Ashford	L/C	13/4/1951	77117
11/6/1951	Ashford	L/C	29/6/1951	79049
30/1/1953	Ashford	Gen	20/2/1953	
11/1/1954	Ashford	L/C	23/1/1964	26700
19/8/1955	Ashford	H/Int	9/9/1955	61887
8/7/1957	Ashford	Gen	10/8/1957	108438
13/10/1959	Ashford	H/Int	31/10/1959	44708
29/12/1960	Ashford	L/Cas	28/1/1961	64938
13/2/1962	Eastleigh	H/Int	10/3/1962	81772
29/5/1962	Eastleigh	L/Cas	30/6/1962	83989

Snodland with 33039 at the head of the 12.03 pm service to Chatham on 13 September 1959. The fireman seemingly having some difficulty in ensuring the injector is working properly.

J.H. Aston

Ashford shed on 16 June 1949 and with the last of the class numerically, C40 posed in the sunshine. Notice only one smokebox handrail has been fitted, a second one was added later. Axlebox tests were carried out on this engine from Ashford in May 1948 on the advice of O.V.S. Bulleid, again their purpose is not recorded.

Roger Carpenter

C40 / 33040

Built at Brighton and outshopped on 23 December 1942.

Sheds

First shed	Feltham
April 1948	Stewarts Lane
April 1950	Tonbridge
July 1950	?
July 1957	Hither Green
May 1959	Tonbridge
May 1961	Feltham

Tender No.

As built	3179
19/9/1945	3142

Boiler Number

As built	1153
15/11/1949	1172
6/1/1956	1128
26/10/1961	1129

Repairs and Works visits	Works / Depot	Type of Repair	Returned to service	Mileage since last general repair
12/1/1944	Ashford	C	11/3/1944	23520
12/4/1944	Ashford	D	15/4/1944	
19/5/1944	Ashford	D	26/5/1944	
19/9/1945	Eastleigh	A	9/11/1945	61630
28/11/1945	Eastleigh	D	28/11/1945	
6/9/1947	Ashford	C	9/10/1947	39986
29/4/1948	Ashford	C	23/6/1948	51052
15/11/1949	Ashford	A	15/12/1949	81570
26/5/1952	Ashford	H/Int	13/6/1952	59819
18/11/1953	Ashford	H/Int	4/12/1953	89790
4/8/1955	?		10/8/1955	
6/1/1956	Ashford	Gen	2/2/1956	130641
6/4/1956	Ashford	Return?	6/4/1956	631
14/3/1958	Ashford	L/Int	3/4/1958	40517
13/10/1959	Ashford	L/Cas	31/10/1958	79356
27/4/1960	Ashford	H/Int	28/5/1960	90749
28/9/1960	Ashford	N/C	5/10/1960	97286
26/10/1961	Eastleigh	Gen	2/12/1961	121056
27/2/1963	Eastleigh	L/Cas	23/3/1963	20191

Withdrawn 14 June 1964.

33038 broadside at Ashford shed in late September 1963. Most of the class achieved mileages of around the 450,000 to 500,000 mark during their lifetimes or in the order of 2000 miles per week based on 48 weeks service per year.

Chapter 6

CONCLUSIONS

In an attempt to analyse or otherwise review the success of the Q1s over their 20-plus years of existence, it is first necessary to look back to the time when the class was introduced in 1942. In so doing though, it is perhaps difficult today to fully-appreciate the perilous situation in which the Southern Railway found itself at such a bleak period in the history of this island.

The need for new motive power at this time can hardly be doubted, and increasing demands upon the railway network for the transportation of men and equipment meant that modern, more reliable, freight engines were a necessity that few could argue against.

What may be argued, however, was whether or not this particular design had any merit. At a time when control of the whole railway system was in the hands of the Government, it might have been more prudent to provide a design more acceptable to the Chief Mechanical Engineers of all the main-line companies, and of a type which could be multiplied piecemeal to operate over the whole network. It seems slightly strange that at a time of national crisis, individual identities and preferences were permitted to continue rather than working together for the common good. Surely, what was needed was a design more suited to a wider variety of traffic, in a way that the later Riddles 2-8-0 would score, and likewise the Stanier 2-8-0 (a number of the which were built by the GWR at Swindon, in a fine example of wartime co-operation).

The Southern Railway had always been in the situation where its abundance of passenger workings meant that there had never been a desperate need for a heavy freight locomotive. Probably the nearest equivalents were the LBSCR K class 'Moguls' of 1913, but the SECR and LSWR were content to pursue 0-6-0 designs, which were equally at home on passenger and freight workings.

C22 under repair at Eastleigh on 20 September 1947 and four days in to what was then classed as a 'D' repair. Most major repairs were carried out at either Ashford or Eastleigh, indeed Brighton did very little work with them. Other repairs being undertaken at the various major depots.
H.C. Casserley

A missed opportunity had surely occurred in 1938 with the Maunsell Q class, the 0-6-0 design being perpetuated at a time when, elsewhere, it had already been considered long redundant as a standard freight engine. Regardless of the state of health of Maunsell (which might explain a conservative approach being taken) the design team missed its chance to look towards the future - a future which, with war clouds gathering, meant that even the most short-sighted must have realised that here was a chance to design a larger, and more modern steam freight engine. After all, a modest increase to the 2-6-0 wheel arrangement had been considered preferable on the LBSCR some 30 years earlier.

But that is not to say the Bullied Q1 was in any way a failure, rather the reverse. In terms of power to weight ratio, the design was a success, but how much more could have been achieved by a 2-8-0? The challenges presented to the operating department in handling trains hauled by a locomotive of such greater power, however, would have been another matter.

In practice, the Q1 was the only Bulleid steam design not to be unsuccessful and unreliable as originally conceived. Of course there were modifications over the years, but these were largely minor, and the only major criticism that could be justifiably levelled at the original design related to the tender construction, where (as recounted previously) the original tenders were rebuilt some years later.

On the subject of braking, or rather lack of it, the Q1 could have handled trains far in excess of those regularly worked had they been fitted with continuous brakes, and it must remain a matter of regret that steam power generally never benefited from what was surely a long-overdue policy to equip all rolling stock in this way.

Whether the design was ever truly intended to last the average 40 years of steam engine life, as conceived, is also open to conjecture. The fact the smokebox wrapper also had to be replaced implies that the original concept may well have been for a functional machine intended to serve its owners for a limited period, that period being perceived as the duration of hostilities.

Subject to the necessary replacement of the smokebox, the whole class

continued to give valiant service throughout the 1950s. Never once was one involved in a major accident or derailment, although there were of course odd brushes in sidings, depots and the like. One of these occurred at Eastleigh steam shed when a former Southern 'Mogul', which was driven from the right, departed the shed at the same time as a Q1, driven from the left. Neither driver noticed the presence of the other, and with both firemen no doubt suitably occupied, the predictable result was inconvenient rather than spectacular.

With steam destined for early decimation, it only took a major fault to develop for the first of the class to be condemned - 33028 was the victim, a cracked cylinder the cause. The remainder slowly fell by the wayside as repairs became due, so that by 1966, only three remained, and these would be gone in the first few months of that year.

Fortunately the British Transport Commission had identified the importance of preserving a member of the class as part of the national collection, and the doyen of the class, 33001, was selected. It presently resides on the Bluebell Railway, and is the sole survivor.

Had the demise of steam not been so accelerated, it is likely that the class could have continued working well beyond the 1960s. Whether men would have been prepared to continue working with steam is another matter, further discourse on which would be to enter into a debate on the social and economic revolution which has occurred since that time. Suffice to say that the Q1 design was a typical product from the brain of a brilliant, if at times eccentric, mind. The fact that aesthetically today, 60 years after its birth, the design still commands comment and admiration can only be a tribute to the builder, and confirms him as one of the most controversial designers in British locomotive history.